Tender Mercies

FOR TOUGH MOMENTS

A 31 Day Journey into the Blessings of God

TERESA E. NELSON

Dedication

To Patty and Lora-jean
who always believed
and always prayed

To My Family
Whose patience is remarkable
Support admirable
Love irreplaceable

Table of Contents

Acknowledgments

To the team who supported the launch of this book,
a sincere and enthusiastic "Thank You!"
Your support and responses made all the difference.

~

To the Self-Publishing School, Sean and Chandler,
a most sincere expression of gratitude.
What world-changers you are!
You make the dreams of writing books come true!

~

A heart-felt appreciation to my husband,
our children and their spouses
who have sacrificed time together while I wrote.

~

A special hug to the nine precious grandchildren
who give me inspiration to keep working for a better tomorrow.

Introduction

In today's drive-though, fix-me-now world, people are facing a multitude of troubles and are demanding fast answers. People are searching for solutions to real-life problems, and they are grasping at things that cause more confusion and insurmountable stress. In the quest for finding significance and belonging, people have found mainstream methods to be dull, overused, and sometimes harmful.

Nothing appears interesting, exciting, or long-lasting. Hope is something to be pursued, but never possessed. Love is an ethereal fog, escaping right before it is grasped. Peace is temporary, or at least something like it pacifies—until the next crisis. Even fun is fleeting, and people of all ages yearn for something of substance between the feel-good parties and the hurried vacations.

When the merry-go-round of mad living comes to a halt, the spinning leaves a residual nausea that's renewed by backward glances of regrets and disappointment.

And for some people, life has thrown them a curve-ball. They hear themselves saying, "I never saw this coming my way!", or "What a shock!" Illnesses, accidents, relationships gone bad, rebellious children, job loss, natural disasters, grief, and so much more, can pick up someone's world and set it down in a swirling mess.

But now there's *Tender Mercies for Tough Moments*. It is a 31-day Blessing Book and Bible study which tackles real life challenges and emotions, offers spiritual solutions, and gives down-to-earth uncomplicated prayers. This book offers sustaining strength, practical insight and the peaceful assurance of God's presence and power.

It looks beyond the natural, and brings in the supernatural God when people can't bear their situation another minute. Within each chapter is a blessing, meditation and a prayer to help calm the anxiety, comfort the hurting and /or counsel the confused. Hopefully, each chapter will draw them to the One who knows them best and loves them most.

The Bible references qualify the blessings. Pertinent questions challenge the reader to search the Scriptures, and if permitted, allow the Holy Spirit to draw them into deeper truths and weightier wisdom. It can turn the focus from self to Spirit, problem to Providence, and despair to the Divine.

Tender Mercies for Tough Moments has a format that is thoughtful, yet quick. In the middle of a busy schedule, an aspiring career person can take a minute and regain his/her focus by reconnecting to God.

A teen-ager can read a blessing and find the courage to face the challenges of high school peer pressure.

A single mother living on little can receive encouragement from the book, and be confident that God will supply all her needs as she leans on Him.

After 30 years of teaching, life-coaching, and ministering to people in need, I have determined that all people need daily inspiration.

When I work with people who face the ravages of poverty, I see the desperate hollowness that aches for a better way.

When I sit with cancer patients, I see the pleading in their eyes about the hereafter.

When I teach incarcerated people about the Bible, I see a hunger for the thing that will help them make better choices and give their lives significance instead of shame.

When I preach to a congregation, I see people who want more. More of God.

When I search the Scriptures, I see Jesus reaching out to real people with real needs. People are no different now than they were then. It is a humble, heart-touching marvel to witness the power of changed lives, to see people go from fear to faith, from weakness to wonder.

For several years I have written weekly blessings on social media. Many people have responded with comments such as, "This is just what I needed for today.", and "Thank you. Now I know where to turn."

Marie wrote, "Thanks so much! Very encouraging", and Wanda said, "This blessing made a real difference in my workplace today." Michael responded by saying, "Keep writing. Where's the book? I really need this."

So, I wrote the book. *Tender Mercies for Tough Moments* is a handbook of hope for all people. But especially . . .

I write for the lost, the inmate, the homeless, the disenfranchised, the alienated, the marginalized, the hopeless. I write for people who cannot dare to rise from the dirt pile and see a different outcome than today's reality.

I write for the individuals whose lives are held in the bondages of abuse, addiction, and lies, by a childhood no one should have, by the grip of poverty, and by absolute anger against God and everyone else.

I write for the victim, the single-mother, the abandoned dad, the woman or man divorced not of their own choosing, and the one widowed way too young. I write for the one whose child has left them heart-broken, and the one whose self-disappointment has turned to self-hatred. I write for those who fear everything and everyone.

I write for the one who has been over medicated, over analyzed and under-loved. I write for none other than the people Jesus came to save, heal and deliver.

The book is to bless those who have no one to bless them.

It is for all who want to walk the road of blessing with their Creator.

Pick up this book and be drawn into a fresh perspective. Dig a little into the Word of God to discover what God is saying to you for the day, and for your current dilemma. Read a daily blessing and discover that it's just what you needed.

If you want to help someone, give them a copy of *Tender Mercies for Tough Moments*. Their difficult life perhaps could use a blessing, a prayer and a glimpse of God. You would be gifting them with a means to their long-lasting hope.

It is my prayer that this book will be used to point people straight to God. Please don't keep it to yourself. Spread the joy. Share the inspiration.

I invite you to delve into the pages of this book. Do what time permits. Read a blessing, meditate on the Scriptures and answer the questions. Say the prayer. Start each day with God, and become established in His goodness, for He has intentions of grace prepared just for you. Don't miss them. Begin the journey today.

To your peace,

Teresa E. Nelson

Day 1

First, We Pray

Blessing

May you be drawn by God himself into the sacred place of prayer. Listen carefully to the Spirit who calls you to this meeting room of grace, and swiftly follow Him there. It is the secret chamber where you and God will converse, and where He waits with a heart full of blessings prepared especially for you—His beloved.

May you heed the tender call to pray as often as you hear it, for this beckoning left unnoticed will become quieter as time passes. You do not want to miss Heaven's invitation to meet with your God and experience His intimate goodness to you.

May you experience the joy of praying first. Just as the sun rises first for each day, may you rise to pray before the duties of the day demand your nonstop time, every ounce of your energy, and every expanse of your mind. Before any situation overwhelms you, may you recognize there is a power greater than you that awaits your humble requests, and find your way to Him.

May you take your situations to the all-knowing Creator of the Universe. God is very well-acquainted with your problems and knows the very best answers for you. It is through your prayers that He rolls up His sleeves, and gets to work on your behalf. His solutions are exponentially better than anything people attempt, and your situations in His hands will also be handled far beyond anything of your own making.

May you witness the Lord of Lords and King of Kings personally and intimately answer your prayers with great precision and perfect timing. Praying first will give you less time to spend in agonizing prayer, begging for help over something He wanted to fix a long time ago. Trust Him.

Because you pray first, may your worries cease, your stress decrease, and your faith increase. Allow the Holy Spirit to call you to this place of powerful exchange between you and God. May you be blessed beyond measure because you obediently and habitually pray first. It is the gateway to peace.

<u>Meditation</u>

<u>Isaiah 55:6-9</u>

Seek the Lord while He may be found;
Call upon Him while He is near.
Let the wicked forsake his way
And the unrighteous man his thoughts;
And let him return to the Lord,
And He will have compassion on him,
And to our God,
For He will abundantly pardon.

"For my thoughts are not your thoughts,
Nor are your ways My ways," declares the Lord.
"For as the heavens are higher than your ways
And My thoughts than your thoughts."

    1.   When are people to call upon God? _____

_____

2. How does God respond to the one who returns to Him?

_____

3. How do mankind's thoughts and God's thoughts differ?

_____

<u>Read Jeremiah 33:2-3</u>

4. How is the Lord identified in this passage? _____

_____

5. What is His promise to us when we call on Him (pray)?

_____

<u>Read Daniel 2</u>

6. When Daniel's and others' lives were at stake, what is the first thing he did? (verse18-19) _____

7. When God answered their prayers for help, what did Daniel do? (verse 19-23) _____

<u>Read Matthew 19:26, Philippians 4:13</u>

8. What is the difference God makes in a situation? _____

_____

9. Can He do it for you? _____

10. What impossibilities in your life can you bring to God for His strength and solution? _____

_____

_____

Prayer

Dear Father,

You draw me to yourself with such tender care. Even though I know it's best to pray first, so often I don't talk to you before I do my own thing. And then I find myself in yet another big mess.

I'm tired of trying to fix everything by myself and then finding myself in the aftermath of my weak and ineffective efforts. Yet, your love hovers over me continually and your watchful eye is ever on me. You are wonderful beyond description.

Will you please prompt me to pray first about everything? I know if I do, all things will be under your orders, and directed to a better end. Would you enter my world and make the difference only you can?

I know without you I can do nothing, and with you all things are possible. You are a powerful, miracle-working God, and you hear my prayers.

So here is my life and its problems and concerns. (List them here. Share with God.) Oh, sweet Lord of my life, help me to trust you with your answers, and believe that they are orchestrated for my very best. Teach me how to wait on my knees, and while I'm there, worship you as the Holy God you are.

I invite Divine solutions, Heaven's power, and the Holy Spirit's presence in every single moment of every single day. Praying first, praying in the middle and praying at the end is how I want to live.

Until I see you face to face, Jesus.

In Your name I pray, Amen.

Day 2

In a Relationship

<u>Blessing</u>

May your relationship with God be your utmost priority and your deepest joy.

This relationship will impact all other relationships in your life.

It is the most needed and often the most neglected.

It is the most desired, and unfortunately, sometimes the most discarded.

This relationship can be the most precious of all, and is often the most unpopular.

May your relationship with God be your hearts' delight and the deepest craving of your soul, because you are His extreme delight and the recipient of His tender mercies.

Since before your occupation in your mothers' womb, God the Father, God the Son, and God the Holy Spirit has celebrated you. God says you are the apple of His eye and rejoices over you with singing.

You, His creation, are His "why". You are why He sent His Son Jesus to earth. You are why Jesus chose to suffer and take your sin upon Himself, set you free from it, and completely forgive you. You are why He gives you the Holy Spirit to comfort, teach, encourage and guide you.

May your relationship with God be your most cherished possession of all. May you guard and nurture this gift with all your heart, soul, and strength. For without this tender and intimate companionship, you falter in faith, or you may love lesser things, and your heart may break.

May you be so overtaken by His love for you that you long for more of it. It is within this sacred ache, you seek the purpose for your life; that is: to experience His love and Presence in every breath you take. He is your Chief Shepherd and Lover of Your Soul.

May this yearning for Him be satisfied in the Presence of prayer, in the Truth of His Holy Word, the Bible, and in the comfort of the Holy Spirit. In these places you can experience the sweetness of His grace and hear His whispers of affection toward you. It is in His loving embrace where contentedness will find its home, and the yearnings for more will finally be satisfied.

May you personally witness the extravagant elation of loving God in return. He longs for your worship and your wonder of Him. In everything you do, seek His glory. Do it not out of duty, but out of delight. Wake each day with the awesome realization that you have been rescued and redeemed by God Himself, and give Him all the gratitude and glory you can.

May you center your life around Him and serve Him. Apply the power of His Holy Spirit to the impossible things in your life. Stand amazed when you see His miracles take place, and worship Him with all your heart.

May your relationship with God be your first love. May all other things pale in comparison. As the world looks on, may people see a life-giving, hope-filling, grace-giving glow of difference. It's the undeniable look of God's love. What a relationship!

Meditation

Read and prayerfully ponder these Scriptures.

<u>Psalm 17:8</u> *Keep me as the apple of the eye, hide me in the shadow of your wings.*

<u>Deuteronomy 32:10</u> *He found him in a desert land, and in the howling waste of a wilderness; He encircled him, He cared for him, He guarded him as the pupil of His eye.*

<u>Zephaniah 3:17</u> *The Lord your God is in your midst, a mighty one who will save; He will rejoice over you with gladness; he will quiet you by his love; he will exult over you with loud singing.*

<u>Jeremiah 1:5</u> *Before I formed you in the womb I knew you, and before you were born I consecrated you; I appointed you a prophet to the nations.*

<u>Romans 8:38-39</u> *For I am convinced that neither death, nor life, nor angels, nor principalities, nor things present, nor things to come, nor powers, nor height, nor depth, nor any other created thing, shall be able to separate us from the love of God, which is in Christ Jesus, our Lord.*

<u>I Peter 2:25</u> *For you were continually straying like sheep, but now you have returned to the Shepherd and Guardian of your souls.*

<u>Jeremiah 31:3</u> *The Lord appeared to him from afar, saying, "I have loved you with an everlasting love; Therefore, I have drawn you with lovingkindness."*

<u>John 3:16</u> *For God so loved the world, that He gave His only Son, that whoever believes in Him should not perish, but have eternal life.*

1. How did God prove His love to the world? (<u>John 3:16</u>) _____

    _____

2. Do you believe that you are loved by God? _____

3. Which verse speaks most to you? _____

4. What are the things that God does for mankind/you? _____

_____

5. Is there anything that can separate you from the love of God? _____

6. What are your thoughts and feelings toward Him? _____

_____

Prayer

Dear Beloved Jesus,

Your love for me is beyond description in language known to man. How great is your love! I am in awe that you would create this world for me, and am overwhelmed that you would suffer and die for a broken, needy, vile sinner like me.

I am shaken with the thought that you think of me day and night, and that you desire my company and my friendship. How can I be, in all my failings, your very hearts' desire? How can I be so loved by you? You have such a compassionate heart for people like me. I don't deserve your love, but you have always loved me.

Yet, I cannot bear the thought of a day without you, and even the thought of going another minute without your Presence causes me to tremble. Where would I be without your love?

Jesus, I want to stay forever in your loving embrace! Show me in your Word and by the Holy Spirit, how to experience your loving-kindness today and always. I love you.

In Jesus Name, Amen.

Day 3

Blessings and Cursings

Blessing

May you choose wisely what you believe and how you live. Every day decisions are set before you in every area of your life, and each decision has its beginning and its ending. How you begin will determine how you end.

May your decisions be for the things of life which God has set before you. In His goodness, He has given you free will. You could choose the things of death, but the promised graces will not be yours.

May you see in every sunrise a promise of goodness destined for you, and know that God has His blessings purposed for you. Know that God, who created the beauty of a pink-orange-purple streaked sky, desires to bring you the lavish beauty of His love today.

May you choose the promise of love. Loving God, obeying God and clinging to Him will bring you a length of days not otherwise known, according to His Word.

May you choose the things of which blessings are made for yourself and for others. Seek God's favor and protection in all you think, say, or do. When you think, allow the thoughts of life and blessing to be in charge; when you speak, speak life and kindnesses to all; when you work, work to God's glory.

May you believe God's promises to you, rather than man's curses and lies. There is no evil planned by God, for God is love. God's Word brings life; whereas curses bring darkness and death. When you curse someone, you are heaping evil itself upon them—and yourself, and it will bring good to no one. When you live in the world of curses, you blindly pursue false gods, believe evil lies, and attract dark and destructive forces to invade your life.

May you take God at His word. His Son, Jesus, said, "I am the Way, the Truth, and the Life." Follow Him. It is the best decision you will ever make. End well.

Meditation

<u>Deuteronomy 30:19</u>

I call heaven and earth to witness against you today, that I have set before you life and death, the blessing and the curse. So choose life in order that you may live, you and your descendants, by loving the Lord your God, by obeying His voice, and by holding fast to Him; for this is your life, and the length of your days . . .

1. How has God blessed you today? _____

   _____

2. In what areas are you choosing life? Death? Blessing? Curses?

   _____

3. What are some promises in the above passage of Scripture?

   _____

   _____

4. Where are you witnessing the power of God's love? _____

   _____

16

Numbers 6:22-26

The Lord bless you, and keep you;
The Lord make His face shine upon you,
And be gracious to you;
The Lord lift His countenance on you,
And give you peace.

5. This blessing is commonly used as a benediction. What are the things requested of the Lord for Israel? _____

_____

_____

6. Are these things available to you? _____

Isaiah 41:10

So do not fear, for I am with you; do not be dismayed, for I am your God. I will strengthen you and help you; I will uphold you with my righteous right hand.

7. Do you believe this promise for your life? _____

8. How has God strengthened you in times of fear? _____

_____

_____

9. Are there places in your life which need your blessing instead of cursing? _____

_____

Prayer

Father in Heaven,

The deceptions of Satan have overtaken me and left me flailing in a sea of confusion, dread and fear, and spewing embittered curses of darkness. I have swallowed the lies, and blindly lived in the bondages of evil day after day, night after night.

It is to be no more. You are calling me to life. I place myself before you and seek your blessing. I choose all the treasures of life that you set before me. Reveal to me, please, the strongholds in my life and break them from me. You are the power of love and freedom, and faith in you is the way to victory in a world held captive by Satan's snares.

Help me to seek your words of blessing, and discard the lies and words of destruction which I have been harboring in my heart. Replace those harmful beliefs and words with the promises of your Word, which is the very essence of sweet healing to my troubled soul.

Guard my mouth when I speak to people, and let me speak words of encouragement and inspiration which build up people, rather than tear down and destroy them. Fill my heart with your peace and grace, so my tongue can be a powerful instrument of good in this world.

I choose you. I choose life and not death. I choose to purposely position myself in the way of life - your way - for me and my family. I desire to faithfully love, willingly obey and enthusiastically embrace you for the length of all my days. It is so very good.

In the Name of Jesus, my Savior, Amen.

Day 4

New Growth in Your Spiritual Garden

<u>Blessing</u>

May you have the courage to turn over the hardened, unplowed sections of your soul.

May you invite God to dig up the dormant, weedy, tough and stiff-necked parts which are covered with pretend smiles and fake joy, and prepare them for planting. Though they may be overgrown with fear, bitterness, and other false protectors, allow God to pull the weeds and plow the hardpan of your heart.

Satan has a destructive field planned for your life which will yield no good thing. His planting will reap a life of misery and pain if given permission. Look to God for your spiritual grounding, and flee from evil's ruin.

When the soil of your heart is prepared for sowing, ask God to plant seeds of knowledge, wisdom, love, goodness, and all His virtues. Set them deep, and let them germinate with the warmth of God's grace. Fertilize with prayer.

May you work every day in your newly seeded plot. Pull out any weeds, such as selfishness, revenge, and bad thoughts. If you let them get big, they are harder to pull. Sometimes the stems break, and the root remains in the ground. Then the weeds grow back quickly and overtake the garden.

May you allow God to rain righteousness on you. As rain softens soil, may God rain upon you, and prepare you for new growth. Let God soften you with a desire for the right thing. That kind of wanting doesn't come naturally from our flesh and is gained only by a submissive spirit.

May you find special delight in the harvest God prepares for you. Your happiness will increase when you see yourself blossoming with kindness where you normally would have brought turmoil.

You will be smiling both inwardly and outwardly when you see God grow patience and wisdom in you where you would have naturally demanded selfish, instant gratification. You will be amazed when you see yourself blooming with love where you would have reaped bitterness and tears.

May you be keenly aware that you reap what you sow. What you put into your world will come back to you in larger proportions. If you just gossip a little, it will come back to be a big deal when the wrong person hears it. If you say something good about someone, it can never come back to haunt you. If you sow peace, your world will be filled with peace.

May you become a bouquet of blessedness to all you meet. Permeate your environment with a joyful spirit, a thankful heart, and a kind soul. It will reap benefits throughout all your days.

Meditation

Sow with a view to righteousness,
Reap in accordance with kindness,
Break up your fallow ground,
For it is time to seek the Lord
Until He comes to rain righteousness on you.

1. With what viewpoint are sowers to sow and reap? _____

    _____

2. What part of your life (heart) is untouched (fallow) by God?

    _____

3. What is it "time" to do? _____

Read Matthew 13:1-9, 18-23

4. In the parable of the sower, the good soil is the heart ready to
    receive God's Word and reap a harvest. Is your heart ready to
    receive the seed of faith, the Word of God? _____

Read Galatians 6:7-8

5. What do you reap if you sow to the flesh? To the Spirit? _____

    _____

6. Are you prepared to witness firsthand the power of God in
    your life? _____

21

Prayer

Spirit of the Living God,

I am ready to have a garden sown to you. It appears my garden is overgrown with the weeds of selfishness and greed, and choking on the thorns of anger and bitterness. Row after row of indulgences and insults thrive alongside the mounds of rebellion and callous existence.

You are calling me to a harvest of the kingdom of God. You are reminding me that I need to allow you to turn over the places of my heart untouched by you. These cold, tough spots need your working and weeding. I need you to break the hard ground of my heart, heal it, and groom it for the planting work of the Spirit. I plead with you to soften me and prepare my whole soul for your purposes.

Dear God, my heart is ready to receive whatever you have for me. Plant within me whatever it is that you want to plant. Then rain some righteousness on me! I will stand here and enjoy your master gardening in me. Go ahead, plow and pull, rain and grow.

Grow within me a crop of goodness, kindness, humility, generosity, courage and love. Weed out the distractions and earthly desires that are not from you, and prepare a harvest of your calling.

How I want a harvest of the right things! Let it be, dear Lord, let it be.

I pray this in the name of my Creator, Jesus Christ. Amen.

Day 5

Fighting the Battles

<u>Blessing</u>

May you heed God's powerful and irresistible invitation to surrender the battles you are fighting over to Him, the Most Victorious Warrior! If you are warring against things impossible, and are seemingly losing day after day, year after year, pay close attention.

May you hear God's command written in Ex. 14:14. "I will fight for you," declares the Lord, "You just need to be still." In the noise, confusion and emotions of the fight in which you find yourself, take this verse to heart. God wants you to find rest in Him while He gets to work fighting for you and your needs.

May you remember that you belong to Jesus Christ. You are His child and He bought you with His shed blood and sacrificial death on a cross a long time ago. Now He lives to bring you to a victorious life with Himself as your Savior and your King.

May you come to the work of surrender. He is aware you are fighting against your own flesh and hell's demon forces all on your own, and is waiting to hear your plea for help—and your abandonment to Him. It's an odd thing to give up so that you can win. But it is the truth of God.

May you find yourself entering a quiet place of peace in the middle of the battle around you. Remember Jesus sleeping calmly on the boat in the raging storm. His disciples were terrified of the wind as the waves swarmed around them; and they thought they were going to die any minute. Not so with Jesus. His inner being was as calm as a glassy sea, for He is peace.

May you remember that in His Presence, you can be unruffled and free of fear, because He is a Mighty Warrior. He defeated death. He has power over evil. He says that with Him all things are possible. (He can handle addiction, cancer, divorce, rebellion, mental illness, abuse, child rebellion, poverty, fear, loneliness, homelessness, doubt, and so on.)

Your part is to stop trying to fight these battles all on your own. Hand over your wrestling with people and problems to the Creator of the Universe. He will fight for you. His Angel-Armies are waiting for His command to get to work on your behalf. Trust Him.

May you look forward to the day when Jesus Christ returns as a Mighty Victor! He is coming on a white horse and His name is Faithful and True. The final battle will be fought, and He will win over the forces of all evil forever! The armies of heaven will rise up and follow Him. And we will dwell with Him forever. This is the ultimate victory! Be at peace.

<u>Meditation</u>

<u>Read I Samuel 17:47, II Chronicles 20:15</u>

1. According to David, Jehoshaphat and God, to whom does the battle belong? _____

2. What are the battles that you are facing as you read this devotional? _____

   _____

   _____

<u>Zechariah 4:6</u>

Then he answered and said to me, "This is the word of the Lord to Zerubbabel saying, 'Not by might, not by power, but by my Spirit', says the Lord of hosts."

3. How was Zerubbabel able to access strength to finish building the temple? _____

4. How are believers to face challenges? _____

<u>Read II Corinthians 1:3-11</u>

5. How is a believer to become calm before the Lord and in their own soul? _____

6. Who comforts us in our afflictions? _____

7. Who delivered Paul (the author) from the great peril of death? V. 9. _____

8. Does God intend for us to be alone in our struggles? What is our part in relation to the struggles of others? _____

   _____

9. Who is struggling that you can pray for now? _____

   _____

<u>Read Psalm 59:9-10</u>

10. Who is with you? _____

11. What is His desire for you? _____

12. Who is your stronghold? _____

Prayer

Dear Mighty God,

Your powerful Word says you have battalions of angel warriors ready to do battle on my behalf. Please give them notice that they are about to be deployed! I am struggling with these things: (list here). I have waged war on my own for countless days and years over things great and small, and it seems I'm battle fatigued, and I am no further ahead than when I started. And sometimes I just lose the fight altogether.

God, would you command all the forces of heaven to engage their weapons and ferociously strike down all agents of evil staged to defeat me? Would you give a battle cry that causes the demons to tremble and run? Would you create strategies that would confuse the enemy and stifle all his efforts?

Would you develop winning tactics that leave victory as the only option? You are God. I have read of battles won miraculously in the Bible. Now I believe that you will fight for me, and victory will be mine over temptation, evil, and my own fleshly desires.

Thank you that you are the One who defeated the curse of death, and determined your people to have an overflow of grace and power. I call unto you to set your unique plan of triumph into gear for me and my loved ones. I place my faith in you, Almighty God.

Thank you that you are the Great Commander in Chief of all the Universe! I'm awed that you love me! I am one of your kids, and I am asking you to bring me to a sure victory.

Thank you for this moment of stillness before you. I sit quietly before you and surrender all my challenges to you. I listen and gently hear in my spirit that you are surely my God, and give you thanks.

In the name of the Son of God, Jesus. Amen.

Day 6

Horrible Fears and
Excessive Tears

Blessing

May you receive from God all the strength and mercy you need to navigate this day and all it holds. If you have crippling fears and excessive tears, know full well that God has his eye on you every second. He hears your pleadings for help for He is God, and He keeps His word. When He says He will never leave you or forsake you, He means it. The Lord is your Rock, your Fortress, and your Deliverer.

May you step forward into your situations, firmly believing what He says in His Word, instead of the lies that you hear in and around you. Get to know the promises and power of God more than the pithy platitudes and awful attitudes of the world. Satan wants you weak. God will make you strong.

May you be ferociously brave. Though your knees shake, your heart pounds and tears stream from your eyes, focus your thoughts on what is currently going on and what God can do, instead of what "might" happen. Fear is a false prison. It is an untrue belief (a lie) appearing to be real, and it deceives you.

May you ask God to reveal to you the deceptions that hold you captive to this monster of fear. It is the truth that will set you free! He is a bondage breaker! He is a defender of His people! He is the empowerment of His kingdom's inhabitants! Let Him take control and be amazed at His strength within you!

Use your fear as a super-agent of change, rather than the paralysis-maker that it wants to be. May you boldly face "I'm too afraid to . . .", and "I can't" and turn these lies into "If God is for me, who is against me?", and "I can do all things through Christ who strengthens me". Believe and live these truths as your banner of victory.

When you lay your head on your pillow tonight, may you survey the day and see what provisions were made and what you overcame. No doubt you were given extravagant grace to handle the challenges, and handed Holy Spirit fortitude to kill the giant of fear. May you give thanks and sleep well tonight.

Meditation

<u>Philippians 4:13</u>   *I can do all things through Him who gives me strength.*

<u>Romans 8:31</u>

What then shall we say to these things? If God is for us, who is against us?

   1.   Where does the author get his confidence? _____

<u>Read Psalm 27</u>

   2.   King David was afraid for his life many times. What did he ask and desire?

         a.   Vs 1 _____

         b.   Vs 4 _____

         c.   Vs 7 _____

        d.   Vs 9 _____

        e.   Vs 11 _____

        f.   Vs 12 _____

3.   What did he believe when he became afraid?

        a.   Vs 5 _____

        b.   Vs 6a _____

        c.   Vs 13_____

4.   What was David's conclusion for fear? Vs 14 _____

_____

5.   In what ways does fear stop you in your tracks? _____

_____

6.   Where have you believed something might happen that never did happen? Did it prevent you from doing something? _____

_____

I Timothy 1:7

For God did not give us a spirit of fear, but of power, love and a sound mind.

7.   What can believers expect from God? _____

_____

8.   Where in your life can you put God's Word to work and overcome fear? _____

_____

Prayer

Dear God,

I am so afraid of so many things. I worry about what is happening, what has happened and what might happen. I have based my life on "maybe" instead of the absolute truth of your very Word and character.

Show me where I am not trusting you and then deliver me from the lies that hold me captive. Release in me a sure confidence in you and your ways. Help me to solidly believe that nothing will separate me from your love, and that I am more than a conqueror in all things I fear and face.

Today, I am afraid of these things. (Tell God of all your fears and your responses to them, and take time to be still as you surrender these fears to Him.)

Empower me by the mighty movement of the Holy Spirit within me and around me to overcome these things. Wipe away my tears. Stop the quaking of my soul, and place my feet on solid ground. I cannot slip with You as my guide. You are my Rock and my Fortress. In you will I trust.

In Jesus' strong name, Amen.

Isaiah 41:10

Do not fear, for I am with you; do not anxiously look about you, for I am your God. I will strengthen you, surely, I will help you.

Day 7

Uncommon Courage

Blessing

May you be a person of God's courage today! May you handle the challenges in life with a spirit of adventure and hope, and place fear and doubt where it belongs—under the feet of Jesus.

May each challenge build resolve and grit, and bring you to your next calling. It may not be easy, and it most likely will be knee shaking, or at least heart-pounding. Without the tricky emotions and daring testing, you will not experience the growth you so desire. It is when you are being painfully stretched, that you become more than you can ever dream. Keep going.

As you rise to new God-directed heights, may you bravely look ahead as you put the past behind you. You were created to be a unique and powerful representative of your Creator, Jesus Christ. He is your firm foundation and is completely trustworthy. Seek His perfect will for you today, then place your faith-feet on the solid Rock and go forth.

May you hear your calling and follow it no matter what the obstacles are before you. Though giant things may threaten you on every side and the terrain be rough, keep going! Listen to the voice of the Spirit and step out as you are guided. Grip and use the Bible as an ever-present compass. It will not fail you. Live the way of the Word of God passionately and boldly. Live as one who is fully prepared for the next challenge. Rise-up!

May you be aware that God has the Warriors of Heaven stationed to battle for you. Call on Him to engage them and be not afraid. With the power of Almighty God at your disposal, you will live as a conqueror! You will overcome! March onward!

May you live in this power today: No matter what, you are totally loved and protected by God. He's got this.

Meditation

Joshua 1:1-9

Verse 9

Have I not commanded you? Be strong and courageous. Do not tremble or be dismayed, for the Lord God is with you wherever you may go.

    1.   To what did God call Joshua? _____

    2.   How was Joshua to handle this new assignment? _____

             _____

John 16:33

These things I have spoken unto you, that in Me you may have peace. In the world you have tribulation, but take courage, I have overcome the world.

    3.   Why is it possible to "take courage"? _____

             _____

<u>Psalm 27:14</u>

Wait for the Lord; Be strong, and let your heart take courage; Yes, wait for the Lord.

4. How are we to handle the assignments we are given by God?

    _____

5. How do we access courage? _____

Prayer

Dear God,

I am often very afraid of things. I often turn and run away, self-medicate, or ignore the whole ordeal. Sometimes I am downright terrified. Since I have no nerve of my own, I ask you for the "guts" to do the right things, the best things, and the wisest things.

Help me to step into the frightful and unknown circumstances of my life with bold valor, and the unbreakable resolve to completely trust you.

Help me to address frightening things with surprising bravery instead of certain cowardice. When God calls me to serve Him, add to my inner being tremendous strength and uncommon courage for every situation.

How I want to valiantly follow you! May I rise to every challenge with a strong confidence in you, the Lord of the Universe. You will accomplish what you call me to be—Free and Fearless!

In Jesus powerful name, Amen.

Day 8

Self-Pity Party

Blessing

May you become aware that feeling sorry for yourself easily gets you messed up as a Christ-follower. The enemy of your soul wants you to focus so completely on yourself that you forget the love of God and the needs of others. The longer you gaze into the mirror of self, the more prominent self-pity and self-gratification will stare right back at you.

May you take a good look at any habit-forming, destructive thoughts of self-pity and recognize them as from the enemy of your soul, and not from God. Perhaps they are disguised as righteous self-indignation and covered up with a blanket of anger. Satan would have you adorn yourself with these things, for in doing so, you feel justified and your self-sorrow will grow.

May you inquire of God to take off any blinders of self-pity you may have. When feeling sorry for yourself, the suffering of others becomes obscure and unimportant, and your own problems look larger than they truly are. It is a dangerous possession. It has its own heart-hardening, depression-forming personality, and wants to keep you all to yourself.

May you go to God with this slippery slide of sin. Confess it, and ask Him to remove this sulking faith-choker, spiritual deadener and hope stealer from your life! Confess the covert comforters of self-pity such as gossip, drugs, pornography, over-eating, shopping, excessive entertainment, media involvement, and more.

May you begin to celebrate the gifts and joys already in your possession because of Christ. As you lay aside all the trappings of self-pity, may you see the freedom that is through Christ, and Christ alone. May you look to the cross and see that the One who died for you, (Jesus), has taken those things upon Himself, and has forgiven you. He is offering you freedom and hope, and will give you a heavenly perspective on these earthly entanglements.

May you go from pouting to praise, and from sulking to sanctification. In other words, may God bless you with His transforming power and make you joyful with His work in you. He is the one to help you make good decisions, think good, think uplifting thoughts and give thanks in every situation. Put a song in your heart and a smile on your face!

Meditation

Hebrews 12:1-3

Therefore, since we have so great a cloud of witnesses surrounding us, let us also lay aside every encumbrance, and the sin which so easily entangles us, and let us run with endurance the race that is set before us, setting our eyes on Jesus, the author and finisher of our faith, who for the joy set before Him endured the cross, despising the shame, and has sat down at the right hand of the throne of God. For consider Him who has endured such hostility by sinners against Himself, so that you may not grow weary and lose heart.

1. According to this Scripture, what are Christ-followers to lay aside? Why? _____

_____

2. Is self-pity a sin with which you struggle? _____

3. If so, how does it look, and how is it comforted? (Ask God to identify this for you.) _____

   _____

4. Instead of looking at ourselves as a victim, on whom are Christians to gaze? _____

5. If we consider the suffering of Christ instead of our own, what are we to gain? _____

6. On whose account did Jesus suffer? _____

Romans 15:13

And now may the God of hope fill you with all joy and peace in believing, that you abound in hope by the power of the Holy Spirit.

7. What three characteristics does the God of hope provide when you believe? _____

   _____

8. Can self-pity live in the same vessels as these qualities? Why or why not? _____

   _____

Read Matthew 4:17

9. What was Jesus' first word of ministry while here on earth?

   _____

10. Why do you think this was his first word? _____

_____

_____

11. Is this relevant today? Why? _____

_____

<u>Read Philippians 4: 6-9,13,19</u>

12. As you pray to God for your needs with a thankful heart, what is promised from Him? _____

13. On what things are God's people to think? _____

_____

_____

14. Who will be with you as you practice these things? _____

15. From where do you get strength to overcome self-pity and other burdens? _____

16. Will your needs be met with God? In what storehouse will God get your provision? _____

Prayer

Dear Father in Heaven,

So often I look inward at my own problems and think only of myself. So often I am so sad for myself, and I am frustrated and angry because things didn't turn out the way I intended. Then I am sadder still, and madder still. Because I am sad, I comfort myself with things that hurt myself or others. Nothing is better than when it started, and now is worse.

I come to you, God, because I am needing to lose my self-pity and its associated sins. I attend my pity parties all by myself because no one wants to listen to me whine. I suffer alone in my self-pity. Your Son, Jesus, suffered on a cross in exchange for my eternal suffering. How you loved me like that, I do not understand. But I believe.

Please take from me this sin of self-absorption. Help me to clearly see Jesus' sacrificial work for me at Calvary. Empower me to lay aside all the stumbling blocks upon which I trip, and run a race of faith that is strong and sure.

You call me to rejoice in my relationship with you, for there is no other gift that can compare. As I focus on the glories of Jesus, my heart becomes glad and it is impossible to feel sorry for myself. I repent of my self-pity and seek your Heaven-sized compassion for others in need.

I know I can do all things through Him who strengthens me. Thank you for your promised joy and peace. You are an awesome God!

In Jesus precious name, Amen.

Day 9

Grumbling to Gratitude

<u>Blessing</u>

May you open wide the door of mind-blowing blessings by choosing gratitude, and witness the arrival of God-designed happenings every day. May you become the place where the presence of God inhabits His praises—because of your thankfulness and joy.

May you choose to be a pathway of God's glory in your "I appreciate it" attitude. Slam the door shut on the "I deserve it" expectations, for they are a set-up for disappointment. Exchange grumbling for gratitude and belly-aching for blessing.

Look for gifts great and small and adhere gratitude to them all.

May your prayers be smothered in thanksgiving as you bring your life before God. In the middle of troubles and challenges, find a way to see the gifts of opportunities therein, and not only the dread and pain.

When living in poverty, choose to see true riches in Christ Jesus.

When living with loneliness, choose to give thanks for the love and constant presence of the Holy Spirit.

When illness visits, give thanks for Jesus, the gentle Healer.

When sorrow overwhelms, give thanks for the comfort that only God can give.

When dark shadows invade your space, express appreciation for the light of life, Jesus Christ.

When you have a grateful heart, you will see your sighing turn into singing, your darkness into deliverance, and your problems into possibilities.

And may you find yourself being grateful for lesser things, like soap and water, phones and music, and work and business - and for the greater things, like breath, forgiveness and freedom. And everything between them.

May you discover that a humble and grateful heart before God and man will lead you down new and different pathways which will leave you pleasantly surprised.

May your light be brighter, your steps swifter, and your smile find its way on your face more often when you realize your possessions, your people and your potential are gifts given to you by God.

May your spiritual eyesight improve, and your own spirit hear the Spirit of God whisper His grace over you. His will is for you to be thankful. May His blessings rest upon you.

Give thanks, give praise, give back.

Meditation

<u>Read II Corinthians 11:23-29</u>   Consider the Apostle Paul's life.

1. List the hardships the Apostle Paul experienced. What was his
    attitude in these experiences? _____

    _____

<u>I Thessalonians 5:16-18</u>

*Rejoice always; pray without ceasing; in everything give thanks; for this is God's will
for you in Christ Jesus.*

2. What did he remind believers everywhere to do and be? _____

    _____

<u>Philippians 4:6-7</u>

*Be anxious for nothing, but in everything by prayer and supplication with
thanksgiving, let your requests be made known to God. And the peace of God which
surpasses all comprehension, shall guard your hearts and your minds in Christ Jesus.*

<u>Psalm 107:8-9</u>

*Let them give thanks to the Lord for His lovingkindness, And for His wonders to
the sons of men! For He has satisfied the thirsty soul, and the hungry soul He has
filled with what is good.*

3. Inventory your attitude. Are there areas in which you are not
    feeling particularly grateful today? _____

    _____

4. Are you thankful for the trials as well as the good times? _____

41

Gratitude List

_____

_____

_____

_____

_____

_____

_____

_____

_____

_____

_____

_____

_____

_____

_____

_____

_____

_____

_____

_____

_____

_____

_____

_____

_____

_____

_____

_____

_____

Prayer

Dear Father in Heaven,

Thank you for the sunshine and gentle warm breezes of love that you have sent across my world. I'm grateful for family, shelter, clothes and food. Though I deserve nothing, you have given me so much.

Thank you for the colorful, artistic brilliance of each sunrise and the myriad of stars hanging silently in the sky. Thank you for the towering trees and fragrant flowers of intricate design. Thank you for flowing rivers, majestic mountains and animals of every shape and size.

Thank you for loyal friends, law enforcement, doctors, nurses and firefighters. Thank you for safety and security at a moment's notice.

I am grateful, Lord, for the times of testing and trials, for in them I see you more distinctly. Thank you for tears shed and pleading prayers said, for in them, I submit to you more readily. Thank you for the healing in illness, comfort in the sorrows, and answered prayers in times of crisis.

Most of all, Lord, I thank you for the path of tears walked by Jesus. Thank you for His willful obedience on that sad day when His blood was shed for my sin on a cross of shame. Thank you for the glorious resurrection of our Savior! Thank you that He is my Shepherd, my Deliverer, and my Redeemer. Thank you that He makes all things new.

Thank you for the indescribable gifts of forgiveness and freedom. It is this grace that I cherish most in life. Every day, precious Father, I see your lovingkindness towards me. May others see it in me, and experience it through me.

In the name of the Lord of all, Jesus. Amen.

Day 10

What to Wear, What to Wear

Blessing

May your choices for spiritual clothing be the reflection of Christ. His wardrobe looks good on you, compared to the clothing of the world and the accessories of the devil. It is time to exchange the old rags of sin for garments of grace.

May you be savvy enough to recognize that the clothes of the "old you" have destructive qualities that make you look bad. Immorality, impurity, evil desires, and greed are false idols and will deceptively look good on the hanger, but repulsive on you. Anger, wrath, malice, slander, abusive speech and lying to people are clothes which hang in the closet of evil.

May you take those old clothes and give them to God. Let Him extract them from your closet of faith. You won't be needing them again. Instead, may you wear a heart of compassion, kindness, humility, gentleness, patience, and forbearance. These qualities are quite attractive on you. They never go out of style.

May you wear the accessory that complements every outfit—love. The Scriptures day, "above all else, put on love." All the other qualities are wonderful, and make you look good. But oh, to top them off with love! Then the true character of Christ is revealed in all you are. Look in the full-length mirror of the Word of God and see what you reflect. Look and see if love lives on the inside and shows on the outside. Love always fits perfectly.

Meditation

<u>Colossians 3:10-12</u>

. . . and put on the new self who is being renewed to a true knowledge according to the image of the One who created him—a renewal in which is no distinction between Greek and Jew, circumcised and uncircumcised, barbarian, Scythian, slave and freeman, but Christ is all, and in all. And so, as those who have been chosen of God, holy and beloved, put on a heart of compassion, kindness, humility, gentleness and patience.

<u>Read I Peter 5:5, Job 40:10, Ephesians 6:11</u>

<u>Galatians 3:27</u>

1. With what things does the Bible say to adorn yourself?

    _____

    _____

    _____

    _____

<u>Isaiah 61:3</u>

To grant those who mourn in Zion, giving them a garland instead of ashes, the oil of gladness instead of mourning, the mantle of praise instead of a spirit of fainting. So they will be called the oaks of righteousness, the planting of the Lord, that He may be glorified.

<u>Zechariah 3:4</u>

"Remove the filthy garments from him, "See, I have taken your iniquity away from you and will clothe you in festal robes."

    2.   What things are removed and replaced from a person, so he/she can glorify God?

    _____

    _____

<u>Psalm 18:39, Read Psalm 30:11, Luke 24:49</u>

    3.   What are the things God/Christ puts on believers? _____

    _____

    _____

    4.   How would you get them placed on yourself? _____

    _____

    _____

<u>Revelation 19:13</u>

And He is clothed in a robe dipped in blood, and His name is called The Word of Life.

    5.   In what is Jesus dressed when He returns? _____

    _____

    6.   Do you have a response to that verse? _____

    _____

Prayer

Dear Jesus,

I've been wearing the wrong spiritual clothes all this time. Please take my old rags of sin and self, and give me a wardrobe that reflects your character. How I long to be dressed in your mercy and love!

You are so wonderful! Thank you for the robe of righteousness that you have put on me when I believed. The greatest gift of all is that you would forgive me and cleanse me of all my sins, see me as white as snow, and call me righteous. I cannot comprehend it all! It is so magnificent!

Clothe me with the things of the Spirit in which you delight. Give my closet a makeover with the graces of God. Place upon me qualities that draw others to you and your truth. Let them be gentleness, a quiet spirit, great patience, deep faith, and more.

Help me to choose love and drape it over everything I do. Oh, that it may be Heaven's love, and not the superficial emotions of this world! May God's love overflow within me, and may it be my greatest gift to the world.

My soul is stricken with such awe when I think of seeing Jesus in His robed dipped in blood. Oh, the price He paid and carries as my ransom. Only a King does that! Only a Savior does that! Only my Redeemer does that for those He loves! How I love you!

In your beautiful and powerful name, Amen.

Day 11

More Month Than Money

<u>Blessing</u>

May you be blessed when living in the hard spot of more month than money. As the bills arrive and the cash doesn't, may you take a deep breath and begin to pray. Put fear aside for the moment and place your faith in a caring God, first and foremost.

May you tell Him your every need. Have courage to be honest about everything. Tell Him where you have deadlines, taken sidelines and can't see the gridlines. It's humbling, but necessary. The greater blessings come more often when we travel upon the broken and meek pathways. The roads of entitlement and arrogance lead to poverty of both pocketbook and personhood.

May you discover the blessing of giving when you have little to give. In the world of greed, God's supply comes through upside-down-living. You must give away what you want. To have a friend, you must be a friend. To curb loneliness, you must help someone lonelier than you. To have money, you must give to someone with less money, and/or give to God's work in this world, even if it's just one dollar. Trust Him. He is on your side and is true to His promises to provide.

May you look to God in this situation and see only Him. If you are looking at what material wealth others have or what they do, your peace will be stolen. Stop the comparisons, for your Father in heaven knows exactly what you need.

May you fix your gaze only on Him. Count your blessings. He gives good gifts to His children. Before you know it, you may have a job offer, something to sell, groceries, a gift, a buyer, or a completed resume ready to give to a perspective employer.

May you be grateful for everything, even when it feels like you have nothing. Remember to say "thank you" to God for the new friend you just met, the $5.00 you found, or the ride to work.

May you give thanks for the programs ready to help you with clothes and work, the church who wants to feed you, and the government worker making you jump through unwelcome hoops. Be the one who uncovers the hidden blessings in the hardships. Treasures await in the trial for those willing to search for them.

May you ambitiously pursue the opportunities put before you. Resolve to escape your poverty trap with earnest prayer and hard work. Send all discouragement and despair packing, for they are not of God.

May you counter-punch the lies such as, "I'm never going to get anywhere," with the truth of God who says, "I know the plans I have for you . . . plans to prosper you . . .".

Battle the feelings such as "I am such a loser" with the words of Apostle Paul who wrote, "I can do all things through Christ who strengthens me" and, "We are more than conquerors through Him who loved us."

May you ask God to replace those destructive forces of anxiety with an extra dose of peace and trust in Him while you are in this uncertain situation. Choose to believe that He will do exactly that.

May this day provide you with all you need in Christ. Pursue with diligence and joy all that has been prepared in the heavens for your life here on earth. Live fully!

Meditation

Read Matthew 6:25-34

1. What does Jesus want us to recall when worried about things?

   _____

   _____

   _____

2. What does Jesus tell us to seek? (Take time for personal inventory.) _____

   _____

   _____

3. Do you believe God is keenly aware of your personal need?

   _____

Proverbs 19:17

Whoever is generous to the poor lends to the Lord; And he will repay him for his deed.

Jeremiah 29:11

"For I know the plans I have for you," declares the Lord, "plans for welfare, and not for calamity, to give you a future and a hope."

4. What is God's plan for your life? _____

_____

_____

Read I Kings 17:7-16

5. What did the prophet ask the Widow of Zarephath to do?

_____

6. What was her response? _____

7. What did she have to do first to get her oil? _____

_____

8. What sequence of events happened that allowed her to be fed?

_____

_____

_____

9. The widow believed Elijah's promise and gave him her bread. Do you believe God's promises when He asks you to give? ____

10. Write your experiences of God's provision in your life. _____

_____

_____

11. What things are holding tightly that God may be asking you to release or submit obediently to Him for His re-working?

_____

_____

51

Prayer

Dear God,

I am in need. I've got financial demands and can't seem to pay all my bills. What am I to do? Today, I will say "thank you" for the struggle, because you tell me to give thanks and not lose heart.

I will say "thank you" for the new opportunities you will give me in this time of learning and challenge.

Would you please show me where I need to adjust my spending, and any negative habits I may have developed? I repent of any wrong handling of money and now pray for extraordinary wisdom to do the right things with it.

I realize that you are a generous, loving Father and the giver of all good gifts. Would you show me the way to be God-honoring with my finances?

Would you provide the money I need in the way I need it given? Right now, I have these financial needs. (Tell God what expenses that you need to pay, and ask God for wisdom and provision in those areas.)

And please help me to see beyond my troubles and reach out to help others in need. Show me where or what I should give someone whose situation is larger or different than mine. I am willing.

In the name of my gracious Lord, Jesus, Amen.

Day 12

Conclusions and Comparisons

Blessing

May you truly understand that you are a spectacular one-of-a-kind person, created by God for His distinct purpose and your good pleasure. May you look in the mirror and become thankful for the "you" that you are today, made in the very image of God.

May you guard against the thoughts that come when you compare yourself with someone else. These thoughts will build their own destructive force within you and defeat any dreams that you may have dared to dream. When you begin comparing yourself to someone and thinking that they are smarter, better-looking, richer, faster, and better at things than you, then you are looking at human limitations rather than the supernatural power of God.

May you realize in making comparisons and making negative conclusions about yourself and others, you are also making yourself or others your own God. You are focusing on what you think you "should" be, rather than what God wants you to become. You are looking at others and concluding that God failed you, that He doesn't care about you, or that you have failed God and there's no use in trying anymore.

May you take those lies and put them under the feet of Jesus. It's time to believe the life-giving, hope-building promises of God instead of the life-sucking, hope-killing deceptions of the devil. Satan misrepresents yourself to yourself. God declares over you that He has a hope and a future of goodness prepared for you.

May you choose that truth. There is a certain indefinable joy that accompanies a person who has a realistic picture of themselves, their skills and abilities and their limitations, who then allows Sovereign God to call, form and develop them into His unique and extraordinary purposes. You are no exception.

Meditation

1. What does the Bible say about those who compare themselves? (II Corinthians 10:12) _____

2. Whose favor are you seeking? (Galatians 1:10) _____

3. Are you conformed or transformed? (Romans 12:2) _____

4. How does a person renew their mind? _____

   _____

5. Is comparing a form of judgment? (Matthew 7:1-2) _____

6. How does judgment return? _____

   _____

Galatians 2:20

I have been crucified with Christ. It is no longer I who live, but Christ who lives in me. And the life I now live in the flesh I live by faith in the Son of God, who loved me and gave himself for me.

7. If you are a believer in Christ, and if Christ is living in you, how would your life compare with the world? _____

_____

_____

<u>Prayer</u>

Father in Heaven,

For so long I've tried to be someone I'm not supposed to be. I confess I've compared myself to other people and tried to be like them. I've become so disappointed in myself and always believed I could never be like "them". And I was right.

I was right because you want me to be "me". You want me to live the life you have ordained for me, not someone else's life. You have made me to be a unique gift to the world around me, and am in the business of bringing your creation (me) into the destiny you have prepared. It is exciting to think of what that could be—fun, free, fantastic!

Help me to seek your favor first, and not fret about what others are thinking about me. Help me to thrive in your purposes for me, and live happily there.

Also, help me to accept people as they are – marvelously and wonderfully made by you. I am sorry for the judgements I have put on others, and as I repent of my critical spirit, I ask that I could see people through your eyes.

I ask you to take my life and let it be wholly lived for you. In that, I will be content.

In the name of my Savior, I pray, Amen.

Day 13

The Shame Game

Blessing

May you ask God to battle ferociously for you when guilt and shame plague you constantly and torment your soul. Take the Word of God and put it on yourself and prepare to win! These attacks are by Satan, the enemy your soul.

You belong to an Almighty King who has defeated death! His Name alone makes the devil shudder! Those reoccurring feelings of regret and condemnation are from the pit of hell, and are no longer who you are in Christ Jesus.

If you have given your sinful past to Jesus Christ for His forgiveness, believing that He died and rose from the dead on your behalf, then those sins are washed away. There is no place in your life for reoccurring memories that God chooses to remember no more. Flashbacks that offer no peace (awake or in dreams) are not from God. Why should you let them fester and infect your life?

When you want to go fetal with the weight of it all, reject it. Stand up! Refuse to let old yearnings and debilitating memories of sin overtake you. Old sin can become new sin if it's given breathing space, and can paralyze or kill the God-placed visions within you.

Wear the full armor of God and stop the darts of accusation, the fiery flames of shame, and the arrows of guilt. The shield of faith in a Warrior

God, to whom you belong, will stop those wound-makers in their tracks.

Wear the breastplate of righteousness always, so the forgiven and forgotten sin of the past cannot penetrate your identity as the Righteousness of God, your new name. See yourself as God sees you.

Stand strong! Battle with prayer. Do not fight guilt and shame alone. Stamp out the self-loathing and the rancid remorse with prayer. Tell it all to Jesus Christ, who lives to give you a life of freedom and victory. Remember what is written in the Word of God. You are more than a conqueror in all these things!

Stand strong! Let the past lay at the foot of the cross, and let God shape you into the victorious and glorious believer that He personally designed you to be.

Stand strong! You have a Savior whose love you cannot escape! Jesus Christ is praying for you Himself and there is nothing that will stop Him from loving you. Remain in His love always.

Meditation

Read John 8:1-11

1. What was Jesus words to the woman caught in adultery? _____

   _____

2. Do you think she was ashamed? Angry? _____

3. What did Jesus say to her accusers? _____

   _____

Ephesians 6:10-17

Finally, be strong in the Lord and in the strength of His might. Put on the full armor of God, so that you will be able to stand firm against the schemes of the devil. For our struggle is not against flesh and blood, but against the rulers, against the powers, against the world forces of this darkness, against the spiritual forces of wickedness in the heavenly places.

Therefore, take up the full armor of God, so that you will be able to resist in the evil day, and having done everything, to stand firm. Stand firm, therefore, having girded your loins with truth, and having put on the breastplate of righteousness, and having shod your feet with the preparation of the Gospel of peace, in addition to all, taking up the shield of faith with which you will be able to extinguish all the flaming arrows of the evil one. And take the helmet of salvation, and the sword of the Spirit, which is the word of God.

1. With what do you struggle? _____

_____

2. How are you to stand? _____

3. How are you to be dressed for battle? _____

_____

James 4:7-8

Submit yourselves therefore to God. Resist the devil, and he will flee from you. Draw near to God, and he will draw near to you.

4. What happens when you resist the devil? _____

5. Are you drawing near to God? _____

6. What happens when you do? _____

<u>Philippians 3:13-14</u>

Forgetting the things that lie behind and straining forward to what lies ahead, I press on toward to what lies ahead, I press on toward the goal for the prize of the upward call of God in Christ Jesus.

7. Is it more difficult to look behind or ahead? _____

8. For what is the Apostle Paul pressing forward? _____

_____

<u>Read II Corinthians 5:18-21</u>

9. In verses 19-20, to what does the Apostle Paul say Christ is committed? _____

10. What does the Apostle Paul beg the reader to do? _____

_____

<u>II Corinthians 5:21</u>

For our sake, he made him to be sin who knew no sin, so that in him we might become the righteousness of God.

11. Do you believe you are the righteousness of God? _____

12. Where is Satan buffering you? (Romans 8:34) _____

_____

13. God doesn't hold your trespasses against you, so why do people hold their trespasses against themselves and others?

(II Corinthians 5:19b) _____

14. How can you keep yourself in the love of God? _____

Prayer

Father in Heaven,

I am bothered sometimes by shameful memories of things I've said and done. At times, they just keep popping into my mind. I know that you have forgiven me for all my sins. I have received your forgiveness through Jesus, but I can't seem to stop thinking about all the bad that I've done. I'm so ashamed before you and the people who know what I've done.

Thank you for your promise that nothing will separate me from your love! I know that my past mess-ups have been washed by the blood of your son, Jesus Christ. In Him, I know I have the victory over all things of temptation and sin! For that, I cannot express enough gratitude.

Would you help me stay close to you? So close that Satan and his agents will run away powerless and empty handed? Would you help me put on my spiritual armor, so no devilish schemes can touch me? Help me to remember your words and powerful promises continually, and may they speak louder to me than the voice of shameful memories.

I step forward into your love, your promises and your prize of faith. I know that by faith I have the victory. I will love you forever!

In the secure name of Jesus, Amen.

Day 14

The Painful Past

Blessing

May your past truly become a thing of the past.

May you lay the heavy burdens of the past at the feet of Jesus. They are an awful load for you to bear by yourself. Jesus has carried all your pain (past, present, and future) to the cross and knows it very well. To surrender it to God is a blessing of immeasurable proportion.

May your past haunt you no more. As you are painfully reminded again and again of things said and done, and sorrow, shame, guilt and remorse sweep over you, please remember that these things are not of God. They are from the enemy of your soul—Satan. Dig us some fortitude and tell him to keep your past to himself-in the name of Jesus! Kick his plan to keep you down and defeated right out of your world!

May you remember only the lessons learned from your past, and remember not the things that sadden you. Jesus Christ has a better plan for your life. Remember that He died for *all* your life, including your past. He wants to comfort what is hurting, and redeem what has been broken. Make Him your sheltering place.

May you remember Jesus' humble past rather than your horrible past, if that is the case.

May you eagerly learn the life of Jesus and became acquainted with His suffering. He willingly gave His life in exchange for yours. He paid your penalty, so you don't have to be held captive by sin and its ugly consequences. Let this miraculous truth invade every cell in your being and jump-start a process allowing God to turn your pain into purpose and power. God does things like this in people every day. Now it's your turn.

May this knowledge give you a reason to believe in tomorrow, rather than ruminating over old wounds and stewing in the memories. Often Jesus said, "You are healed. Go, and sin no more." He is far more interested in our new lives with Him, than in the wreckage of days past.

May you take your eyes off the rear-view mirror, and fix your focus on God's promises of goodness in your life. If you keep looking back, you will crash into what is in front of you. Look forward with hopeful, joyful expectation to the next blessing from your Father in heaven. He is always good.

Meditation

<u>Psalm 91:1-4</u>

He who dwells in the shelter of the Most High God will abide in the shadow of the Almighty. I will say unto the Lord, "My refuge and my fortress, My God in whom I trust." For it is He who delivers you from the land of the trapper, and from the deadly pestilence. He will cover you with His pinions, and under His wings you may seek refuge. His faithfulness is a shield and bulwark.

1. Where can you find refuge? _____

2. Who is your great protector? _____

Read II Corinthians 5:17

    3. What is your identity when you are in Christ? _____

    4. What old things do you think have passed away? What former things do you desire to be gone forever from your life? _____

    5. What new things have replaced the old things in your life? _____

Read Hebrews 12:1-3

    6. What things are believers to lay aside? _____

    7. How do we run the race before us? _____

    8. Upon whom do we gaze? _____

    9. Where is Jesus now? _____

Read Ephesians 4:30-32

    10. How are we instructed to respond to those who have caused us small and/or insurmountable pain? _____

_____

Read Luke 23:34

    11. How did Jesus respond to those who crucified Him? _____

_____

    12. Who is God asking you to forgive? Pray, asking for guidance.

_____

Prayer

Dear Father God,

My past haunts me. It sweeps over me at times like a tidal wave, and painful memories visit afresh. There are many times I have wept over someone's cruelty or rejection of me. It still hurts when I think of it, even when these things happened years ago.

So many things happened to me that weren't fair or weren't right. My pain is ever before me. I see it and feel it where ever I go, and it follows me like my shadow.

And there have been several occasions when I have hurt someone. I wish I hadn't said or done those things, and am very sad about them all. My actions have caused misery for people I love, and I wish I could do it all over again with a better ending.

You say to forgive others and forgive myself. So often I've said with teeth-clenched that I would never forgive someone, or never forget what they did. I've held it against them for many years. I can taste the bitterness within me, and I wonder if it is destroying my chance of having any good life.

I know my sins put your sweet Son, Jesus, on the cross as a blood sacrifice. He finished the work He came to do—make a way for people to be forgiven. You offered forgiveness to me through Him. Although I don't deserve it, you forgave me when I first believed. How you must love me!

Would you help me to completely forgive the people who have been treacherous with me, and have wounded me beyond words? I have kept all this anguish to myself, and let it eat away at my soul. (Tell Him your story.)

I now need your miraculous healing. This is too big for me to treat myself. I give you all the heartaches of my past, and ask you to heal them with your love. I am afraid, and know it may take some time. Bring to me the people, the prayers, and the power that will help me to surrender it all to your healing, saving touch. Here I am.

Thank you for being so faithful, so gracious, so kind to someone broken like me. You are God and I will praise your wonderful name forever!

In the healing name of Jesus, Amen.

<u>Notes</u>

Write your own words of forgiveness towards yourself and others.

_____

_____

_____

_____

_____

_____

_____

_____

_____

_____

_____

_____

_____

_____

_____

_____

_____

_____

Day 15

Wounding Words, Winning Ways

Blessing

May you stand strong when your soul is wounded by false and cruel words of family, friends, neighbors, social media, and the world around you. May you remain loyal when your faith in Christ is tested. Even though your first instinct is to fall apart, pay back or run away, God calls you to a higher response.

As chosen treasures of God, may you access the powers of Heaven to help you do the right thing. If you allow Him, the power of the Holy Spirit will guide you to the greatest path of blessing in the middle of this unbearable attack.

May you find your refuge in the shelter of the Almighty. Your Father in Heaven sees and knows what has just happened, and He is waiting with open arms to give you what you need. Run to Him in prayer and tell Him about the injustice, persecution and all the related anger.

May you be obedient to God when you are first fired upon with lies, accusations, and down-right verbal abuse. Offer prayers for your offenders and render forgiveness their way. These are easier said than done, but it is what Jesus showed us by example. Remember Jesus' forgiveness for you and His accusers, and pass it on to yours.

May you recall the persecution of Christ each time you are mocked for faith in Him. He was tortured, beaten, spit upon, lied about, falsely accused, betrayed, crucified and pierced. Identify with His sorrows and His victory. Look at His suffering and see His patience. Look at the cross, and see His love. Look to His burial, and see His resurrection power.

May you be brave and wise by seeking the powerful and counter-cultural words of Christ, your Shepherd. It's not popular, but you are to rejoice when picked on for following Him. You are to look ahead, see your reward in Heaven and trust Him with the moment at hand. Your status in Heaven is eternal, and this agony is but for a season.

Meditation

Read Luke 6:27-38

    1.   Is it possible to love your enemies? _____

    2.   Whose example are believers to follow? Verses 35-36 _____

_____

Read Matthew 5: 11-12

    3.   What are you to do or say when persecuted for your beliefs?

_____

_____

_____

<u>Read Luke 6:31</u>

Just as you want people to treat you, treat them in the same way.

4.   Is it possible to live like that today? _____

5.   Who do you need to forgive for their harsh criticisms or wounding actions? _____

_____

6.   To whom do you need to ask forgiveness for your words or actions? _____

<u>Ephesians 4:31-32</u>

Let all bitterness and wrath and anger and clamor and anger and slander be put away from you, along with all malice. And be kind to one another, tender-hearted, forgiving each other, just as God in Christ also has forgiven you.

7.   Is there any resentment or bitterness in your heart toward anyone? Is it causing you any of the above thoughts or behaviors? _____

_____

_____

<u>Galatians 5:22-26</u>

But the fruit of the Spirit is love, joy, peace, patience, kindness, goodness, faithfulness, gentleness, self-control; against such things there is no law.

8.   Who places these qualities (fruits) within you? _____

9.   Do you want to live by the flesh or by the Spirit? _____

Prayer

Father in Heaven,

It's downright painful when people accuse me of things that aren't true, and say things that are surely meant to hurt me. I want to either scream or cry, hurt them, hurt myself, or at least do something to give myself relief from the pain.

I know you know how this ridicule, false accusations and abuse feels. You went through far harsher treatment than I ever could. Yet you forgave your killers. What a wonderful Savior you are!

Would you help me forgive those people who have said and done these awful things to me? I can't do it on my own. I get tied up in knots just thinking about it.

Thank you for forgiving me for my own sins and my own weaknesses. Your Word is my guide to love my enemies. It tells of your unconditional love for all people no matter what they do. Help me to do the same.

Would you replace my bitterness and anger with thoughts and actions that give you glory? I surrender my sin, and trust that you will replace it with the fruits of the Spirit. Work them in me, I pray.

And in the face of opposition for your sake, I am willing to stand. Would you give me strength and wisdom to remain devoted to you when it happens to me? You are the true source of all sure victory, and you are the power-giver of overcomers. You are my healer, my strong tower, and my deliverer! I cannot thank and honor you enough!

In the name of Jesus, who loves me, Amen.

Day 16

Waiting and Waiting . . . and Waiting . . .

Blessing

May you learn to rest in the Lord and wait patiently for him. Although your circumstance may appear impossible, God has it in His hands. Although you have begged God, bargained with God and blessed God, and there appears to be no answer from Him, He hears you. He hears your prayers and your pleas. It is not too late. It is never too late, for He has eternal ears.

May you trust Him with your life and be free from the fleshly fear that can so easily attach itself. Fear grows when we look at ourselves or others as the source of our solutions. We know our own limitations, and down deep inside, we are afraid that we can do nothing to fix this problem or this person. This is where you look to Almighty God and wait on Him.

May you cry out to God, and tell Him everything. There is nothing like pure honesty before a Perfect God. Tell Him the things for which you are waiting. Tell Him how long you have been waiting.

Tell Him about the child gone astray, the job you can't seem to land, and the relationship that won't get better. Tell Him about the weight you can't seem to lose, the illness that won't be healed, or the tears that just won't stop. Tell Him about the cravings that won't go away, the anger that stirs within your soul, and the fact that you desperately need Him.

May you ask Him for patience to face the day and all that it will hold. Ask Him for belief in His timing that puts your heart at peace. Patience aligned with trust grows deep faith in God, especially in the toughest moments.

May you ask Him for soul-calm as you wait. Soul-calm is what you need when you see others getting their prayers answered ahead of your prayers. Know that His alignment of things in your life is for your good and His glory.

May you trust that in this waiting time you are being made into what He wants you to be-more like His Son. It is in waiting on God that you gain strength and wisdom for what lies in the future. You will then mount up with wings like eagles, run and not get tired and walk and not get weary.

<u>Meditation</u>

<u>Isaiah 40:31</u>

Yet those who wait on the Lord
Will gain new strength,
They will mount up with wings like eagles,
They will run and not get tired
They will walk and not become weary.

Psalm 33:16-22

Behold, the eye of the Lord is on them who fear Him,
On those who hope for His lovingkindness,
To deliver their soul from death,
And to keep them alive in famine.
Our soul waits for the Lord;
He is our help and our shield,
For our heart rejoices in Him,
Because we trust in His holy name,
Let your lovingkindness, O Lord, be upon us,
According to how we have hoped in you.

1. What are some promises for those who wait on the Lord?

   _____

   _____

   _____

Read Romans 9:22-23, I Timothy 1:16

2. How has God been patient with people? _____

   _____

3. Who demonstrates perfect patience? Why? _____

   _____

Read John 11:1-45

4. In Verse 4, Jesus explains the reason for Lazarus' illness and its result. What does Jesus mean? _____

   _____

Prayer

Dear God,

I've been waiting, Lord. I've asked you for so long for so many things, and I haven't seen any answers.

I don't always understand why you answer my prayers the way you do. Sometimes it looks like you don't answer at all. But I know you do, in your own perfect way and in your own perfect time.

You have been so patient with your people and with me. You wait for people to come to you for forgiveness and blessing, and they don't come. So, you wait. You desire a joyful relationship with people more than anything. And you wait some more. How you and all of Heaven must celebrate when your children repent and become a part of your eternal family!

Please give me the ability to wait patiently for you, and know that you have my situations in your control. I choose to believe that you are working all things for my good and your glory. Each day I will trust that you know best and obediently follow your Words and your ways.

Your Word also says that you have your watchful eye on every sparrow. How much more you watch over your people! You have no evil in you. Only love. That is enough.

I adore you, Lord. You are my whole souls' desire, and I long for you. As I wait, I'll just worship.

In the beautiful name of Jesus, Amen.

Day 17

Joy and Happiness

Blessing

May your search for joy bring you to the Joy-giver Himself—Jesus Christ. Joy is an uncommon grace given to you by the God Himself and one that defies explanation. There is a wide chasm between what some people label happiness and what Christians know as joy. Joy is the one that is best pursued.

Happiness is material, circumstantial and earth-bound, and joy is a gift of the Spirit, unfazed by circumstance, and heaven-sent. Happiness is temporary; it comes and goes depending on any given situation. Joy is the promise of an Eternal God, and takes residence within a believer relentlessly, regardless the situation.

If the pursuit of your life is possessions and adventures of this earth only, you will sadly miss the unique, God-given, experience of heavenly joy. If you find yourself caught up in the rat-race of getting ahead, getting high, or getting discovered, you will miss the bliss of joyful giving, joyful worship and joyful service.

May your joy be wrapped up in love. It is joy's prerequisite. It is impossible to be joyful without love. This love is a gift of the Holy Spirit, and originates in the heart of God.

May you receive the forgiveness of God through Jesus Christ. When you do, you receive the greatest gift of love ever to be given. Your sin-debt has been paid in full, and you are released from the penalty of eternal separation from God. Your bonds of death are broken, and you are set free. This is love sown for you, and it reaps joy within the very heart and soul of the recipient. Make it yours.

May you grip this gift whole-heartedly and enjoy God. May you add to your joy by worshipping Him and thanking Him. It is impossible to be a miserable, grouchy, self-obsessed human being while adoring God for who He is, and what He has done. No fancy words are needed, just be yourself when you worship Him.

May you praise Him as the Great King, the Lord of Lords, the Lamb, the Savior of the World, the Creator, the Lover of your soul. Give thanks that He is your Refuge, your safe place, your Redeemer. Thank Him for saving you from your sins, and for giving you His Holy Spirit. Thank Him for His love, His amazing grace, and His provision of the things you have in your life.

Thank Him for trials and tribulations, celebrations and cool refreshment as you pray. When you do, joy will surprise you and find its home in you.

May you add to your joy by living as He would have you live. Seek His good pleasure and walk closely to Him, hearing His whispers of acceptance and gladness about you. You will be smiling and giving the world a taste of super-natural grace.

May you practice confession and repentance as a pathway to joy. These things bring a certain contentedness which calls joy its home. You will not be joyful if you do any of this out of duty, religious piety, or demand. Joy resides where love resides.

May you add to your joy through service. Joy kept to oneself is like a fire without fuel. It will turn to smoldering ashes. Service to God and to others is grace-response, of the heart, of the soul. It is not from duty or demand. It is pure and selfless. Give of your time, resources, treasures, and talents, and be a personal carrier of God's joy.

Lastly, may you remember the joy of Christ. While He was praying for the lost, He was weeping tears of blood. In that agonizing moment, He prayed that the believers would have the His joy. He looked to the joy set before Him. His joy was in the knowledge that He was dying to set people free (Hebrews 12:2). In that truth is true and eternal joy.

Meditation

Romans 14:17, Deuteronomy 32:1-11

1. What did Jesus want His followers to possess? (John 15:1-11)

   _____

   _____

2. According to verse 11, why did Jesus speak these things? _____

   _____

   _____

3. Moses sang a song of rejoicing at the end of His life after 40 years of wandering in a dusty wilderness. How is this possible? (Deuteronomy 32:1-11) _____

   _____

4. In what did he rejoice? _____

5. How was it possible that Jesus had joy when knowing He was soon going to be crucified? _____

   _____

<u>Romans 14:17</u>

For the kingdom of God is not eating or drinking, but righteousness and peace and joy in the Holy Spirit.

6.   How does a person attain peace and joy? _____

_____

7.   What are the works and rewards of serving people?

(Isaiah 58:6-12) _____

_____

Prayer

Dear God,

I feel no joy today. I confess that perhaps I've not been looking to you for real, true happiness. Instead, I've been looking at everyone and everything else. And I haven't been very successful at being happy. In fact, I've been sullen and sour.

I look at you, Jesus, and I ask for the kind of real joy that only is in knowing you. Help me to look past my circumstances and passionately pursue a thriving relationship with you.

Oh, to have a wildly, scandalously blissful connection with You! Oh, to have a foot-stomping, hand-clapping, head-bowing, knee-bending link with God! How could I be so blessed?

And to think, God, that someday I will dance before your throne forever! I'll be joyfully worshipping you with all the lovers of Jesus!

In your ecstatically magnificent name, Amen.

Day 18

Cravings and Callings

Blessing

May your body, mind and soul be satisfied fully with God as you immerse yourself in His perfect love for you.

May your cravings for momentary things be replaced with yearnings for eternal things.

May you be able to discern that the immediate satisfaction of the earthly craving may destroy you, while the reward of your heavenly calling will sustain and satisfy you.

May you discover that the love of Jesus Christ occupying the empty and broken places will bring healing and peace. Be humble and abandon all pride. Invite Jesus Christ into these places of pain. Let Him uncover each layer of failure and disappointment. Trust Him with every wound, and ask Him to touch and heal every single one. Though tears may fall, and you feel like your heart is broken into hundreds of pieces, keep talking to God.

May you keep surrendering your story and your emotions to Him. He will place His healing grace in and over these hard things. Time will pass. Trust will grow and become your pathway to victory. And every second will be worth it.

May you replace the cravings' lies with your Creator's truth. For without God's written words of freedom onto your heart, the call of the cravings will dominate your thoughts and control your actions once again. Talk to God—constantly.

May you tell Him everything. Tell Him how you've tried and tried, but with no victory. Tell Him how your feelings of failure just spur you on to more cravings. Tell Him that in your heart of hearts, you want to win victory over this demon.

May you find tender mercy waiting for you—from God's heart to yours. It will be a sweet balm for your anxious soul. Instead of giving you what you deserve, he will give you what you don't deserve—peace, power, new life, a new heart, open eyes and healthy living.

Ask for more and more of the Holy Spirit's power to be released within you. Ask for the will and desire to stay connected to Him. He will answer you, because He loves you.

Find God's people and stick with them. Some of your friends have their own battles to fight. They cannot help you unless they have been beautifully and miraculously saved by God Himself. God's people will fight for you in prayer and support you when you feel battered by temptation and overwhelmed by life's demands.

Finally, may you discover that the pathway to freedom is not self-determination, but rather humility and surrender. Admit your sins, and release your past, your present and your future over to God. Stop fighting the battle all my yourself. Abdicate all control to Him. He has more love for you than words can describe, and He can be trusted in the tough moments of addictive cravings. In God alone, you will find your power to overcome, your promise of a brighter day, and your purpose of Godly proportions. Trust Him and be blessed.

Meditation

<u>Matthew 29:41</u>

Watch and pray that you may not enter into temptation. The spirit indeed is willing, but the flesh is weak.

<u>Hebrews 4:15-16</u>

For we do not have a high priest who is unable to sympathize with our weaknesses, but one who in every respect has been tempted as we are, yet without sin. Let us then with confidence draw near to the throne of grace, that we may receive mercy and find grace to help in time of need.

1. How do you resist temptation according to Scripture? _____

   _____

<u>Psalm 50:1</u>

And call upon me in the day of trouble; I will deliver you, and you shall glorify me.

2. What is God's promises if we call on him in troubled times?

   _____

3. Do you believe that God loves you? If not, read John 3:16 and know that it is about you. _____

4. Have you been saved by God? If not, read and respond to <u>Romans 6:23</u>, and <u>I John 1:8-9</u> _____

5. Do you have a craving or addiction that is overpowering you? If so, what is it? _____

6. Do you want to be set free from that force? _____

7. Would that be the best time to call on God's people and ask for help and prayer? _____

Prayer

Dear God,

I want to tell you right now that I need to be saved by you. I believe Jesus died for me and took my sins, even my addictions and failures, upon himself. I accept your gift of forgiveness as my own. Save me from my reckless wrong-doings.

Help me to crave only you and your presence. Replace the cravings for bad things to be replaced with a burning desire for good things. Allow me to hear your urgent calling for truthful and right living above my craving's shrill screams to spiral downward. Help me to remain constantly in your love.

Please give me strength every day to face the monster of addiction and deep cravings. Please fill me with your Holy Spirit who can help me overcome my every temptation. Help me to say "no" to death and "yes" to life.

Provide me with people to show me the new way, the best way. I need to know with whom to associate and from whom to flee. Would you put into my path people of wisdom, experience, purpose and prayer? Would you supply mentors to guide me through the tough times? Would you give me teachers to show me truth from your written Word, the Bible? I need your power, Lord.

I believe that you love me, and have a plan to restore my life. I surrender all of me and my entire life to you.

In the saving name of my Savior, Jesus, Amen.

Day 19

School? Homework? You're Kidding!

Blessing

May education be a blessing in your life and not a curse. If thinking about education brings up painful memories of failure, disappointment and anger, it is time to allow God to heal the past and bring you to a place of learning and wisdom. It's worth every bit of work you will put into the process. The rewards will amaze you.

May you first bravely step into the past with an attitude of forgiveness towards teachers, classmates, school officials, parents, and bus drivers who may have caused you pain while attending school. This is no easy assignment. Go to God with this, for it is far too difficult to tackle by yourself. Talk to Him about every single situation, as it comes to mind, and ask for the power and strength to forgive them all.

Ask God to forgive your bitter and hateful thoughts and actions towards them—and yourself. In this difficult groundwork, also forgive yourself for getting distracted by peer pressure, and the behavior that caused you to stop going to school and stop caring about learning. Forgive yourself for thinking you are a failure, and see yourself as God sees you. Forgiven. Redeemed. Ready.

May you replace fear with fortitude. When panic pays a visit, recall that old things have passed away (God has taken care of it), and that God says all things are new. You have a promise of a hope and future with God at the lead. This is true for education as well. Set your mind on what an education will do for you and your family, and get busy.

May you have courage as you enter the promised land of learning. With an improved attitude, a dream for a better life, and God on your side, there is no stopping you. Learn something every day; learn about God, learn from God, learn from books, classes, listening, teachers, experiences, mistakes, successes, and prayer. Life-long learners lead successful lives, and you can be one of them.

Meditation

Read Proverbs 10:14, Proverbs 18:15, Philippians 1:9-11, Proverbs 18:2, Proverbs 2:1-6, Proverbs 3:5-6

Proverbs 9:9-12

Give instruction to a wise man, and he will be still wiser; teach a righteous man, and he will increase in learning. The fear of the Lord is the beginning of wisdom, and the knowledge of the Holy One is insight. For by me your days will be multiplied, and years will be added to your life.

1. Wisdom is many things, including learning knowledge. What do you gain by learning of the Lord, and fearing Him? _____

    _____

    _____

    _____

    _____

    _____

<u>Colossians 2:8</u>

See to it that no one takes you captive by philosophy and empty deceit, according to human tradition, according to the elemental spirits of the world, and not according to Christ.

2. What are some things to guard against when acquiring knowledge? _____

3. How do you find the knowledge of God? <u>(Proverbs 2:1-6)</u>

   _____

4. How does excellence come to you? <u>(Philippians 1:9-11)</u>

   _____

5. What do you think is the difference between knowledge and understanding? <u>(Jeremiah 3:15)</u> _____

   _____

6. What is your next step in learning? Pray for some God-guided goals. _____

   _____

<u>Psalm 119:105</u>   *Thy Word is a lamp to my feet, and a light to my path.*

<u>Psalm 119:11</u>   *Thy Word I have treasured in my heart, that I might not sin against thee.*

7. Why is it important to be also a student of the Word of God?

   _____

   _____

Prayer

Dear Father,

I'm sorry about my attitudes about education and especially about school. I accept your forgiveness for dropping out of school, hating it, and hating the people involved. Thank you for being with me through that very hard time in my life. You know every trouble I had, everything wrong I did, and every injustice that came my way.

Bless the teachers and mentors who taught me in the past. I know they were doing the best they could at the time. Perhaps they didn't always understand what they were doing, and were unacquainted with my struggles and dreams. I choose forgiveness for them.

Help me to choose forgiveness for myself regarding my past educational decisions. I believe I need to take another step towards a better education. Would you show me how, where and when to begin? You have something wonderful for me to learn and share with the world.

I give you my anxiety and fear about the whole thing. I'm ready. I'm so glad that you are going to walk with me as I work toward every goal. Thank you for those who have taught me thus far, and thank you for all the people you will put in my path. You are good.

In Jesus name, Amen.

Day 20

The Power Source
for Temptation

Blessing

May the moments of your strongest temptation become the gateway to your greatest victory. God has set up a system for you to live successfully even when facing the biggest, most fierce temptation. May you tenaciously grip His promise that He will provide you a way of escape. In the early waking moments of each day, may you see clearly God's participation in your every victory.

May you follow the footsteps of Jesus when He was tempted by Satan. Take the Word of God and write it on your heart and put it on your tongue. In the middle of hell's fast and furious attack on Jesus, He always answered Satan, "It is written." You do the same.

May you come to understand that Jesus understands your temptation. He has suffered in all ways you have, according to Scripture. Speak to Him about your weakness, sins and temptations. He has encountered temptation like all mankind, yet He still did not cave to sin. He is the perfect one with whom to share your struggles.

May you be so full of the Word of God that when you feel your flesh getting weak, you stand strong, and you stay strong. Draw from your power source, the Bible, and speak its life-giving, war-winning words over the situation. Declare a victory before the battle even begins. Satan will put his tail between his legs and make a run for his own territory when hearing the words of Almighty God.

May the plans of evil aimed for your destruction never touch you, and may the resources of Heaven planned for your conquest empower you. Your God-designed destiny awaits. Believe in the goodness of God and allow Him to prepare you for victorious living.

May you engage the life-force of Heaven daily in your life . . . that is, the Holy Spirit which resides within you. You will be astonished as you see yourself stepping away from temptation and walking toward righteousness.

Meditation

Read Luke 4:1-13

1. In what ways was Jesus tempted? _____

   _____

   _____

2. What was His response to Satan each time of temptation?

   _____

3. Satan came to Jesus when he had been fasting for 40 days and was very weak physically. Yet He still did not sin. When are you the weakest? _____

   _____

4. How can you still be victorious? _____

   _____

I Corinthians 10:12-13

Therefore, let every man take heed, lest he fall.

No temptation has overcome you but such is common to man, but God is faithful, who will not allow you to be tempted beyond what you are able, but with the temptations will provide a way of escape also, that you will be able to endure it.

5. What will happen if a person thinks they can withstand temptation on their own? _____

6. Will God allow you to be tempted beyond your ability to withstand temptation? _____

7. Do you believe this? _____

8. Have you seen God provide you escape routes when tempted?

   If so, where and when? _____

   _____

Read Hebrews 2:18, 4:15

9. Why is Jesus able to help people being tempted? _____

   _____

Read James 1:12-18

10. What are the rewards of being tempted? _____

   _____

   _____

11. What are the consequences of giving in to one's own desire?

_____

_____

_____

Prayer

Dear Father of Love,

Thank you for the example of Jesus when facing temptation. I'm thankful that He defeated the enemy every time.

Thank you for His prayer which says, "lead me not into temptation".

Lord, you know the areas where I crash and burn. I need your life-giving power to overcome (list temptations here). Be my interrupter of sin, and my deliverer over sin. Stand in the gap and give me a way of escape— every time!

Your written words give life and light in the dark and unknown places. Your words give strength and victory over the most enticing invitations of evil. Your words are a most precious treasure. As I write them on the tablets of my heart, they will be a lamp to my feet and a light to my path. They will be my guide for my entire life.

In the victorious name of Jesus, I pray. Amen.

Day 21

On What to Say and What Not to Say

Blessing

May you rise up today and make decisions that bring goodness into your life and into the lives of others. With the help of Almighty God, may you resist the temptation to speak "your mind" if it is going to hurt someone. May your words be "grace-laced" and your thoughts "mercy-minded" while you go about this days' work and play.

Kind words will come easier if you allow forgiveness to blaze a trail before you. Harboring hurt and holding hatred will block your blessing, because what is in the heart will find its way out of the mouth. What comes out of your mouth will determine the response of others who have influence over your life.

When tempted to gossip, or tear down another human being, pray for Holy Spirit "duct tape" across your lips, if necessary. This will keep you from verbally unloading truck-loads of destructive verbiage on people. Instead, speak words that will build up mountains of hope in the hearts of discouraged people.

May you understand the power of words when speaking to children, spouses, friends, coworkers, and acquaintances. For what you say has the power to change the course of their lives-and yours. Have a gentle tongue, for regrets cannot be found in soft, healing words. And sometimes practice silence, for often it reveals more understanding than speaking.

May you also pay attention to the words God says to you. His words are full of love and wisdom, and were written with you in mind. In the Bible are instructions and guidelines for life; and if believed and lived, will strengthen and equip you for today and all of eternity. Absorb His words, and live by them. Before long, you will hear yourself sharing these words of life and light with someone who desperately needs to hear them.

Be blessed today as you seek the words and ways of God.

Meditation

Proverbs 11:12

By the blessing of the upright a city is exalted, but by the mouth of the wicked, it is overthrown. Whoever belittles his neighbor lacks sense, but a man of understanding remains silent.

Proverbs 15:1-2, 4

A soft answer turns away wrath, but a harsh word stirs up anger. The tongue of the wise commends knowledge, but the mouths of fools pour out folly. A gentle tongue is a tree of life, but perverseness in it breaks the spirit.

1. What harm is brought by a wicked mouth and harsh words?

   _____

   _____

2. Can you remember words spoken to you that were extremely encouraging and complimentary? _____

3. Who spoke them to you and how did those words impact your life? _____

_____

Read Proverbs 18:21

Death and life are in the power of the tongue, and those who love it will eat its fruit.

Read James 3:1-12

4. What kind of power is in the tongue? _____
5. How is the tongue a force for good and evil? _____

_____

Matthew 15:18

The good man out of the good treasure of his heart brings forth what is good; and the evil man out of the evil treasure brings forth what is evil; for his mouth speaks from that which fills the heart.

1. Where do our words originate? _____

Read Isaiah 43

2. What words of life does the Lord speak to Israel and you?

_____

_____

3. How do you feel when hearing these words from God? _____

_____

4. In verse 4, God says you are precious in His sight, and honored and loved by Him. Do you truly believe this? _____

5. Pray, and ask God what encouraging words can you speak to someone today. Write an example. _____

_____

_____

Prayer

Dear Loving and Kind Father,

I am sorry I have said things that were hurtful or discouraging to my loved ones. I am sorry that I have spoken rashly and without thinking first of the outcomes. Thank you for your forgiveness.

Please give me wisdom and grace to say the things that are kind and good. Please give me the power of the Holy Spirit to hold my tongue, for so often I have spewed rotten words.

Place your seal of kindness on my lips, Lord. And place your words deep into my heart. For from my heart, come my own words. Grow within me a garden of grace, dear God. Let it be a place where lovingkindness feels right at home, and where vile words, cursing and gossip can no longer live.

Grow within me a heart of love. Instead of judging people, teach me to speak words that inspire them to make wise choices and live accordingly. Instead of harming someone, let my words bring life and hope to whomever you put in my path. All people need encouragement and hope, Lord. No matter my "mood" at the moment, let your Spirit guide my mouth and stir my heart with goodness.

I read your words, Jesus. You spoke words of compassion to the weary, words of power to the weak, and words of empowerment for the hopeless. Let it be so with me.

In the tender and strong name of Jesus, Amen.

Day 22

Being Royally Ticked-Off!

Blessing

May you take a deep prayer-breath before you say and do anything regretful when you are absolutely, fire-branding furious! May you hold your tongue and your punches when you want to take matters into your own hands and administer your own brand of justice immediately. It is extremely difficult not to do that - when you feel completely justified to do so.

May you learn to walk away from the first feelings of rage. It is not easy when you believe that you have been compromised, demoralized and marginalized! It is not easy to walk away when you are feeling "put upon, taken advantage of, and ripped off". But turn and walk away.

May you learn to surrender your thoughts of payback to the Mighty One who says, "Vengeance is mine. I will repay." Taking matters into your own hands will reap chaos in your soul. The feelings of satisfaction and justice you desire will not come to you. Instead, you will become even more dissatisfied and empty. Revenge has its own reward, and it's not pretty.

May you swiftly turn to Jesus and remember His life! He was mocked, falsely accused, given a set-up trial, traded for a murderer, whipped, beaten, blasphemed, arrested, and put to death. And yet he said not a word. And He could have easily gotten down from the cross and walked away. But He chose love. He chose you.

When you are as mad as a hornet, and seeing red, may you see the red that flowed from Jesus while on the cross. It is this red blood that was shed for you and paid the ransom for your sins. His blood also flowed for the person with whom you are hopping mad, also. His crucifixion was for them.

May you choose the greater way of forgiveness and wisdom when you or your loved ones are being treated in indescribably unfair ways, and your temper is about to explode. Chose truth and love. These are the towers of power. They reside in the heart of God and can be accessed by prayer. Sometimes a wise Christian friend or counselor can help you navigate Jesus' way of handling your infuriating situations and people.

May you examine your underlying fears and pain when you are angry. Allow God to heal and comfort you in these areas and find your peace in Him. Although it is perfectly normal to be angry at times, do not let sin take the wheel and steer you into all sorts of evil. Guard your thoughts, actions and words, and bring them into alignment with the will of God. You will not be sorry.

Meditation

Ephesians 4:6

Be angry, and yet do not sin; do not let the sun go down on your anger, and do not give the devil an opportunity.

1. What is the Lord's directive regarding anger? _____

    _____

Read Nahum 1

2. What is God's response concerning the wicked?

_____

_____

Numbers 14:18-19

The Lord is slow to anger and abundant in lovingkindness, forgiving iniquity and transgression; but He will by no means clear the guilty,....Pardon, I pray, the iniquity of this people according to Thy lovingkindness.

3. What is the nature of God in these verses? _____

_____

4. What makes for great understanding and folly? (Proverbs 14:29)

_____

5. In what does God delight? (Micah 7:18) _____

6. What traits does God wants us to put away? What are traits that God wants us to clothe ourselves? (Col. 3: 1-17) _____

_____

_____

7. How do you walk out your Christian faith in times of anger? (Galatians 5: 14-26) _____

_____

8. Jesus addresses personal relationships, including anger. What did He say about anger and murder? _____

_____

9. Are you angry with anyone, or have a relationship problem regarding an issue with money?

_____

_____

Prayer

Dear God,

Right now, I am ticked off about these things: (list them), and I'm downright smoking mad about (list them). I am sorry I said and done things in out-of-control anger, which brought about more bad than good.

Help me to handle my injustices and hurts according to the way of wisdom and the spirit of love. Allow me to wait for you to work, as I give you all these bad situations. Most of all, set me free from the clutches of anger and rage that control me.

And when I am white-hot mad over injustice, please help me so I have no regrets over how I respond. I pray for your control over my flesh. Let me walk according to the Holy Spirit and reaps its fruit in my life.

With your Holy Spirit presence in me, I will overcome.

In the peaceful name of Jesus, Amen.

Day 23

Grief Work

Blessing

May you seek comfort in the love of God as the tears flow like a raging river and waves of grief hit you like an overwhelming tide. It is not a thing of mystery to Jesus, as He also wept tears of heart-wrenching sorrow. As He stood by the tomb of His friend, Lazarus, the Bible says, "He wept." Not a quiet tear rolling down His troubled face, but more than likely, shoulder-shaking, gut-wrenching man sobs. He knows your heartache intimately and is responding to it even now.

May you find comfort in the promises of God when the words of people seem empty or shallow. Although people who care say well-meaning things, sometimes nothing seems to help. Only the Word of God and the presence of the Holy Spirit can break though the wall of weeping and bring your soul to a place of rest. And during those times when you can't even pray, stay. Stay in the presence of God, be still, and let Him wipe away your tears and heal your heart in ways only He can.

May you linger in the secret place with Him long enough to know His tender Grace Embrace. Those times of life when words aren't enough, and the ache is too deep to explain, Jesus Christ Himself will hold you and keep you. He has mighty strong and righteous arms and can bear your insurmountable load. Nothing is impossible with God.

May you walk the path of peace in the garden of prayer as you do your grief-work. It is in the garden of prayer that you will be given the strength to labor with full-strength sorrow and find super-strength grace to face tomorrow and yet another day after that day.

May you grieve with hope. Sorrow does not travel to the darkest places of desperate despair when a person secures their future with God. In the saddest of sad situations, a Christ follower will find a unique and indescribable comfort in the ways and workings of our eternal God. There is a glorious future to be had; a tearless, bright place of love that will make all things good. It is called Heaven.

Meditation

Psalm 116:15 *Precious in the sight of the Lord is the death of His Godly ones.*

1. Why would the God of the Universe call the death of His own children "precious"? _____

   _____

   _____

Hebrews 9:27

And inasmuch as it appointed for men to die once and after this the judgement, so Christ also, having been offered once to bear the sins of many, shall appear a second time for salvation without reference to sin, to those who eagerly await Him.

2. How many times do people die? _____

3. To whom shall Christ appear a second time? _____

   _____

<u>Lamentations 3:19-25</u>

    4. In what does the grieving person have hope? _____

    _____

    5. What things do you think when feeling sad? _____

    _____

    _____

<u>I Thessalonians 4:13</u>

    6. How does mankind grieve without Christ? _____

    _____

<u>John 11</u>

    7. What was Jesus response to Lazarus' death? _____

    _____

    8. What was Mary and Marth's response to Jesus delay in coming to heal Lazarus? _____

<u>John 11:25-26</u>

I am the resurrection and the life; he who believes in me shall live, even if he dies, and everyone who lives and believes in me shall never die. Do you believe this?

    9. What did Jesus mean when He said, "*Everyone who lives and believes in Me shall never die.*"? _____

    _____

    10. Do you believe He is your resurrection and life? _____

Prayer

Dear Lord,

I pray today for all those who weep over the loss of someone dear to them. (It might be you)

As their heart breaks, wrap them in your blanket of comfort and hold them tightly. Would you be so close to them that they may know beyond of a shadow of doubt that you are there?

In their darkest hours of sorrow, Lord, hold your light of love for them, so they may see a glimpse of hope for the next day. Let not despair overtake them.

Give those who mourn friends to support them and food to sustain them. Provide people to pray passionately for them while they are in the valley of the shadow of death. It is hard work to grieve, and they need grace upon grace when they do.

In their grief, may they lean on you for each painful moment. Bring to their minds the promises of heaven and eternal life, so they can be filled with hope for their loved one, and weep only for a season.

Let your Spirit of rest be upon them. May their sleeping hours be uninterrupted and healing, and their waking hours full of supernatural comfort from your Holy Spirit. May they know your tender mercies in even these, the toughest moments.

In the name of the Risen One, Jesus, Amen.

Day 24

Lost in Loneliness?

Blessing

May you reach out to the One who is able to fill your emptiness and satisfy the desire to be known by someone. May you find the God who knew you before you were born, and cry out to Him, who desires to be your most certain Friend.

May you look and see Him laughing with you, wiping away your tears, and becoming your rock in the most uncertain times of life. May He heal the deep wounds and the brokenness that life has thrown at you.

May He comfort you when you feel the ache of loneliness, even in a room full of noisy people. May He heal the hurts that medication can't touch, and may He fill that isolated and hollow cave where nothing seems to fit.

May Jesus Christ draw you into a certain sacred connectedness when you feel like you belong to no one or no place. May He settle the floating thoughts and emotions that have no place to land, and give you solid footing. May He walk with you, and bring you to the place where you are supposed to be—right at home with Him.

May He quench the fires of loneliness with His Living Water, the fullness of His Holy Spirit. Most of all, may He satisfy the longing for the One to whom your spirit belongs—Himself.

May you ponder the absolute agony of Jesus' most lonely hour. In the excruciating moments of His life, while He was suffering and dying for our sins, He cried out to the Father, "My God, My God, why have you forsaken Me?"

May you reach out to understand Jesus' loneliness. He experienced a total separation from God. It is the single, most poignant example of loneliness on the face of earth for all time. It was necessary, for it became the way for us to never be separated from God ourselves. Because of Jesus death and resurrection, you, (and all of mankind), won't have to experience the wide, terrifying eternal chasm of emptiness and forsakenness. You will never be alone.

Meditation

Psalm 147:3   *He heals the broken hearted and binds up their wounds.*

Psalm 73:23-24

"Nevertheless, I am continually with you; you hold my right hand. You guide me with your counsel, and afterward you will receive me to glory. Whom have I in heaven but you?"

Psalm 27:10

For my father and my mother have forsaken me, but the Lord will take me in.

Psalm 27:4

"This one thing I have asked of the Lord, that will I seek after; that I may dwell in the house of the Lord all the days of my life, to gaze upon the beauty of the Lord and to inquire in his temple."

Psalm 73:25-28

Whom have I in heaven but Thee? And besides Thee, I desire nothing on earth. My flesh and my heart may fail, but God is the strength of my heart and my portion forever. For, behold, those who are far from Thee will perish; Thou hast destroyed all those who are unfaithful to Thee. But as for me, the nearness of God is my good; I have made the Lord God my refuge, that I may tell of all Thy works.

1. What is the Lord to the Psalmist when he was stricken and alone? _____

2. What is the Psalmist's greatest desire? _____

   _____

3. When everything was gone, and there was nowhere to turn, where did the Psalmist go? _____

4. Have you ever felt forsaken by God? _____

5. Does God forsake His own? _____

6. What have you done to help yourself in times of loneliness?

   _____

7. Where could you go to receive comfort in loneliness? _____

   _____

8. When all is said and done, what does the Psalmist say is the only thing he has? _____

9. Is this true for mankind? _____

Prayer

Dear God,

So often I find myself all alone, and my heart nearly breaks from loneliness. I long for companionship that would be longer than just a day. So many times, I wish for someone who would stay by my side, and let me share my life with them.

Now I understand that you are the One for whom I have been yearning the entire time. You became ultimately forsaken and alone, so I could know your Presence always. That is so amazing and too big for me to really understand. But I believe.

Come to me now, I pray, and be my closest companion. Fill my lost and longing heart with your love and comforting friendship. Thank you for being closer than a brother; and thanks for your promise to never leave me. What a wonderful friend you are!

In the name of my ever-present Savior, Jesus, Amen.

Psalm 23

The Lord is my shepherd, I shall not want.
He makes me lie down in green pastures;
He leads me beside still waters.
He restores my soul;
He guides me in the paths of righteousness
For His name's sake.
Even though I walk through the valley of the shadow of death,
I fear no evil; for Thou art with me.
Thy rod and Thy staff they comfort me.
Thou dost prepare a table before me in the presence of my enemies;
Thou hast anointed my head with oil;
My cup overflows.
Surely goodness and lovingkindness will follow me all the days of my life,
And I will dwell in the house of the Lord forever.

Day 25

Wiped Out Wilderness

Blessing

May your winter season be a time of soul-rest from the arduous tasks of harvest, employment and just getting through the too busy, too demanding seasons and holidays. May you go to God with your "wiped-out" wilderness that has left you numb, exhausted, and broke.

May you allow God to give rest to what is weary, fill what is empty, and supply warmth to what has grown cold.

There is a special kind of rest to which God calls people. It is a promise known only by those who know and adhere to the good news of Jesus Christ. It is a soul-rest from over-work and striving; and set by God Himself for believers to imitate. The Bible says He rested on the seventh day after He completed His work of creation.

It is entered by allowing God to take the "I can't take another step" kind of fatigue that you carry, so He can prepare your tired body, weary mind, and edgy emotions for new plantings of faith and beauty in the spring.

It is entered by allowing God to stop you running in your tracks, so you can sit in His presence and refresh.

It is entered by allowing God to close off the noisy demands of life, so you have time to read His Words and hear them in your heart.

It is entered by allowing God to close your eyes, so you can see more of Himself and less of the world.

It is entered by allowing God to take the places of your soul which has grown ice-cold or frozen by life's unrelenting blasts, and thaw them with the full warmth of His forgiveness and lovingkindness towards you.

In this sacred rest, may you receive a supernatural blessing and know that you have been restored by God Himself. May you be revitalized in work, satisfied in your soul, and once again passionate in your purposes.

Meditation

Hebrews 4:1-13

1. Are you in need of a Sabbath rest? _____

2. Why is this important? _____

_____

Matthew 11:28-30

Come to Me, all who are weary and heavy-laden, and I will give you rest. Take my yoke upon you and learn from Me, for I am gentle and humble in heart, and you will find rest for your souls. For My yoke is easy, and My burden is light.

3. Jesus is willing to carry your load. What will you find in His presence? _____

_____

_____

4. What loads are you carrying that make you very tired? _____

_____

_____

5. How does one enter eternal rest? (Revelation 14:13) _____

_____

6. How does "dying to self" give you rest? (Romans 6:1-12, 20)

_____

_____

7. Where do you go to "Be still and know that He is God?"

(Psalm 46:10a) _____

Prayer

Dear God,

I'm tired and worn out, and exhausted with life. So many things make me feel "run down" and "run over". I've been working extremely hard on many things. From morning to night, I'm checking off the list of things I must get done. Sometimes during the night, I wake up to write down more things to do when I get up in the morning. I need a break!

There are so many demands. Doctor's appointments, employment with overtime, family obligations, school, car maintenance, paying bills, shopping, and more keep me in motion from sunrise to deep into the night. Holidays drive me crazy, because then life gets even busier.

There are so many emotions that make me fatigued. Sometimes guilt weighs heavy on me. Sometimes the thought of not getting everything done frightens me. Sometimes the expectations of others anger me when I'm doing the best that I can. Sometimes the disappointment in myself saddens me.

You say to stop. You say to find the kind of rest that only you can give. You say you give refreshment, redemption and relief. How I long for that!

It's not easy for me to step off the merry-go-round, Lord. But I will—with your help. I will come fighting and kicking perhaps, but I will come and sit in your Presence and receive your message to me today.

You, the Creator of the Universe, rested—yet I do not. I desire to enter your Sabbath rest. I know it is a strengthening, empowering rest which will protect me from disobedience and fraying at the edges.

Bring me to that sacred place. It is where you will soothe my furrowed brow, calm my trembling nerves, and slow my pounding heart. It is where you will give me undisturbed sleep and peaceful days.

Your restful place draws me into repentance and washes me as white as snow. It is where you take my burdensome guilt and give me a refreshment from the rivers of grace. Take me there.

Your holy ground of rest is a place where you will relieve me of the world's demanding expectations and revive me with a focus on Heaven's purposes. Keep my heart from becoming numb in all my striving for success. Prompt me to trust you with all things and fret not.

What a loving Savior you are! You know I need rest, and have called me into it. Here I come.

In the sweet calm of Jesus' name, Amen.

Day 26

Losing Life and Getting It Back Again

<u>Blessing</u>

May you take a chance and consider what people say about Jesus is true. If you have avoided anything "religious" because you think religion is not for you, stop and see what the One and Only God has for you.

May you take a serious look at the stories of people in the Bible and see your common ground. The Bible characters had human needs, just like you. Then Jesus came to their world and changed their lives in miraculous ways. He can do the same for you.

May you be brutally honest with yourself and God. And if you are desperate to stop the bleeding in your life, then take a good look at the man, Jesus Christ, and how he saved and healed people with their broken lives. He can do the same for you.

May you learn from the woman who had been bleeding for twelve years. Her only solution after that horrible time was to get to Jesus. Her life had been sucked dry of health, happiness and hope. She was desperate to get to Jesus. He was her <u>only</u> hope. He is your only hope, also.

May you risk the mocking of friends and family to know Jesus and receive His life-giving, soul-saving touch. He risked everything and gave up His life for you to have a real, abundant, joy-filled, hope-filled life.

Now He lives to give you the things you cannot get for yourself.

Now may He heal your weary soul, your sick body, or your confused mind as you reach out in belief that He can. May you experience His total forgiveness. May you be set free from the ravishes of sin and illness. May you hear His calling and receive His peace.

May you fall at Jesus' feet and tell Him everything about your life. May you trust Him with your story, your survival and your sin. When you are real about your bleeding life and your need for Him, as the woman described in Mark Chapter 5, He will compassionately forgive you and take you into His family as son or daughter. It's too good to miss.

May you listen for His whisper of peace. It will come. May you hear him say the same words He spoke to the woman. "Go in peace." It is the best way to live.

Meditation

Mark 5: 25-34

And a great crowd followed him and thronged about him. And there was a woman who had a discharge of blood for twelve years, and who had suffered much under many physicians, and had spent all that she had, and was no better, but rather grew worse. She had heard the reports about Jesus and came up behind him and touched his garment. For she said, "If I touch even his garments, I will be made well." And immediately the flow of blood dried up, and she felt in her body that she was healed of her disease.

And Jesus, perceiving in himself that power had gone out from him, immediately turned about in the crowd and said, "Who touched my garments?" And his disciples said to him, "You see the crowd pressing around you, and yet you say, 'Who touched me?'" And he looked around to see who had done it. But the woman, knowing what had happened to her, came in fear and trembling and fell down before him and told him the whole truth. And he said to her, "Daughter, your faith has made you well; go in peace, and be healed of your disease."

111

1. Look at the desires and needs of your life, and list them below. Have they been brought to Jesus? Are they Godly pursuits or worldly strivings?

   _____

   _____

   _____

2. What things have you done for answers and/or progress in your needs or wishes? Have you tried everything and still feel defeated? Perhaps like the woman in the story, you are more broke, sicker, lonelier, sadder, and without hope? _____

   _____

   _____

3. How did the woman's future look before she met Jesus?

   _____

4. How would you describe your future? _____

   _____

5. In the long run, does it matter what others think or say? _____

6. Are you willing to risk temporary ridicule for an eternal experience of healing and deliverance from the very Savior of the World? _____

7. Is peace something you desire? How would you attain it? _____

   _____

Prayer

Dear Jesus,

How I need you today! My life is down to the last bit of hope. I keep messing up, and keep thinking something will change. Now I realize that it is a powerful touch from you that I need.

I come to you with the whole truth about everything. Help me to hold nothing back from you.

(Talk to God about your life, your troubles and your needs. Take your time.)

How wonderful you are! Thank you for shedding your blood on the cross in exchange for my bleeding life. You were desperate to save me long before I was desperate to be saved by you. You gave your life for me, and I love you for that sacrifice.

I reach for you now, Jesus, and ask for your healing. Would your healing power touch all the places within me that have been broken, crushed or empty? Would you take my desperation and turn it into a sincere delight to be alive? Would you place your spirit of hope within me and give me moments where I am joyfully surprised by you?

I am asking for your Holy Spirit strength to face each day, as I lean confidently on you, and depend less upon my own ways. Would you meet my current real-earth needs as only you can? Thank you for your answers to this prayer.

In the healing, saving, life-giving name of Jesus, Amen.

Day 27

The Things of Success

Blessing

May you be blessed with exponential success. May you super-glue yourself to the very pillars of success and hold fast and true to these values. The world defines success as achieving power and accumulating money. God defines success as loving Him with all your heart, soul, mind and strength.

May you reach success God's way. It is brought about by being:

- Rooted in prayer before God.

- Grounded in the Word of God.

- Directed by the Spirit of God.

Success God's way brings the best results, and it is something you don't want to miss.

May you be prayerful before Him. Spend time in prayer with God, who has your destiny in His hands. He desires to bring you to a place where you are utilizing the gifts He gave you, enjoying His presence in your life, and where you will experience real, wide-awake progress.

May you experience the prayer room where your battles are fought and won, hearts are healed, and answers are given. It is where God enjoys your company, hears your needs and engages all the angelic forces of Heaven to bring you to where you need to be.

May you be <u>formed by His Word</u>. The Holy Bible is full of actions and attitudes that any believer can put into practice. May you become an avid reader, and an ambitious doer of all the instructions written there. These principles, if applied, will bring you to heights never dreamed or imagined.

May you allow yourself to be malleable in the hands of God, through His Holy Word and by His Spirit. You will be amazed at how life changes, because you change. At times your journey may be difficult, but being available to God's working will bring you to the very best outcome.

May you be <u>guided by His Holy Spirit</u>. Allow God to fill you with the wonder-working power of His Holy Spirit. Listen to His promptings in your own spirit. The more you obey God, the louder you will hear His voice. Ask God to add His "super" to your "natural", and hang on for an eye-widening, jaw-dropping, heart-pounding ride of faith!

You will see yourself being a blessing to others in unimaginable fashions, and you will know beyond a shadow of a doubt, that it is none other than God! You will have new and different dreams which will grip your heart and motivate you to greater heights. You will accomplish them for God's kingdom's sake and your own good.

And be thankful. When there is no gratitude, there is no gracious giving. Without giving, the heart becomes lifeless and brittle. When a heart is brittle, it's easy to break. A broken heart cannot succeed on its own. It needs God to heal it again. So be grateful and live accordingly.

Meditation

Psalm 20:7

Some boast in horses, and some boast in chariots, but we will boast in the name of our Lord.

1. What are some things that people trust more than God in today's culture? _____

   _____

   _____

I Peter 5:6

Humble yourselves, therefore, under the mighty hand of God, that He may exalt you at the proper time, casting all your cares upon Him, for He cares for you.

2. How does a person get promoted or honored? _____

   _____

Read Jeremiah 18:1-6, Isaiah 64:8

3. What is the meaning of "You are the potter, I am the clay"?

   _____

   _____

4. In whose hands do believers let themselves be shaped? _____

   _____

   _____

5. Are you willing to be workable clay in the hands of God?

_____

_____

Read II Timothy 3:16

6. How does the Scripture say Scripture is to be used? For what does it bring gain? _____

_____

John 6:63

It is the Spirit who gives life; the flesh profits nothing; the words that I have spoken to you are spirit and are life.

7. What does the Holy Spirit do in a person? _____

_____

Mark 8:36

For what does it profit a man to gain the whole world, and forfeit his soul?

1. How important are riches and other things termed "successful" by the world? _____

2. Are there times in your life where riches and success were of the greatest importance? _____

3. How can a person forfeit their soul in this regard? _____

_____

Prayer

Dear God,

Show me what true success is, and let me prosper in the path you have destined for me. Let the lustful lure of the world's success fade in my heart, and prepare in me a pathway of success by your design.

Give me the strength to develop the disciplines of prayer, Bible study and listening to the Spirit. For in doing so, I will be a powerful testimony to your greatness and glory.

Your Word, the Bible, is the place where you have put the way to wisdom. Open my heart and mind to absorb all the instruction written there. Give me a new understanding and an enthusiasm for all the history, parables, songs, directions and Divine guidance as I turn each page. It is truth for living.

Take my life and teach me to be willing clay in your hands. Shape me according to your will, not mine. Guide me by your Spirit. I pray that I can sense each nudge and instruction it gives and quickly obey.

Teach me what I need to know, show me what I need to do, and bless me according to your perfect will. Thank you.

In the Name of the Father, the Son and the Holy Spirit, Amen.

Day 28

From the Bad Place
to the Best Place

Blessing

May you rise up, even though you are sinking low. May you rise up into the fullness and power of God's love. You are to lay in the depths of despair no longer. There is God. He sees you, and desires to bring you from bondage into freedom.

He is calling you to step into the joy-destiny He has ordained just for you. Even though you cannot even dare to think there is a better life, hear His tender, pleading whisper of invitation. "Come unto me, all who are weary and heavy laden. My yoke is easy and my burden is light" is the message for you from the Savior, Jesus Christ. There is hope. He has seen your tears and heard your groanings, and is no stranger to your pain.

May you experience the presence of God in the agonizing lonesome moments of your situation. In the silence soul-screams of "Who cares? Does anybody care?", know you have not been forgotten. He cares and is faithful to His own Word, which says, "I will never leave you or forsake you." He cannot abandon you. You are His child.

May you come to wholly accept that you are His beloved. After a life-time of hearing and believing just the opposite, it is time to take God at His word. He writes, "I have drawn you with lovingkindness", and "You are precious in My sight." Hear the prophet Jeremiah declare the words of God, "For I know the plans I have for you. Plans for welfare and not for calamity, to give you hope and a future."

May you come to see beyond the darkness of despair into the Light of Life. If you see no change ahead for a long time, and you dare not believe that you will be delivered from your situation, then it is time to look toward Jesus, who is the Way, the Truth and the Life.

He is the Deliverer, the Fortress, the Rescuer, the Strong Tower. If you are thinking "I'm never going to get out of this", or "Nothing is ever going to change", hand that over to the One who makes mountains move, who puts the stars in place, and who died and rose from the dead to save you. Take the lies here on earth and exchange them for the truth of Heaven.

May you take your current dilemma and despise it not. Let God turn your bitterness into betterment, and your fear into faith. Who knows, perhaps you are here for such a time as this. Often the hardships are avenues to greater purposes. In the middle of a storm, it is impossible to see the rainbow. But it will come. In the middle of your brokenness, it is impossible to believe there is blessing. But it's there. Roses will bloom again.

May you rise up and step out. This matter may be your responsibility, and perhaps it is time to take courage and act. There are those who will support you (Ezra 10:4). Trust God always. Even today.

Meditation

Psalm 142:7

Bring my soul out of prison, so that I may give thanks to Thy name.

1. What does the Psalmist plan to do when the Lord delivers Him from his captivity? _____

2. How does God declare His love and protection to Israel? (Isaiah 43:1-13) _____

   _____

3. Can you believe He will love you in the same fashion? (Psalm 69:33) _____

4. How does God respond to the needy and to His own who are in prison? _____

5. According to Isaiah 43:18-19, is it possible to put the past behind you? _____

6. What new things does God say He will do? _____

   _____

7. In Genesis Chapters 37-45, Joseph was in prison unfairly and for a long time. Yet at the end of the story, we see God's purpose in all of it. He saved his entire family from famine.

   Read and learn from this story. Pray and ask God to reveal His purposes for you in due time.

8. What do the prisoners do in Jerusalem when they are set free? (Psalm 102:18-21) _____

9. Rewrite <u>Romans 8:28</u> in your own words. _____

_____

_____

_____

_____

Prayer

Great God,

Would you bring me from my bad place into the best place?

Would you turn my broken-ness into blessed-ness? My hurts into hope?

You are the One who can take a person in the deepest pit and place their feet on the highest peaks, according to your Word.

For people in their toughest moments you generously lavish tender mercies upon them. For those who fragile, you fortify with your power.

You can turn anyone's agony and angst into an awesome adventure with you.

The sinner, you save; The crying, you comfort; the lost, you love.

You can do anything, for you are God! I praise you that you redeem the hard things of people's lives, turning them into good things that are beyond anyone's wildest dreams. Thank you that you will do the same for me.

In the name of Jesus, my Redeemer, Amen.

Day 29

An Unexpected Refreshment

Blessing

May the times of absolute fatigue, emotional turmoil, basic burnout, and blasé weariness be completely replaced with a satisfying refreshment that gives rest, energy and passion for a new day.

May you be courageous and resolutely set on finding the life-source you so desperately need. If you're working hard, worrying hard, and wishing hard, and still you find exhaustion of body and soul a daily companion, then consider Jesus for your answers. Nothing else will work.

May you stop and unload the heavy load of life, its sins and sins' baggage, at the feet of Jesus. Bold as that statement may be, it is the act of repentance to the Savior, Jesus Christ, that will bring release from guilt, shame, regret, anger, bitterness, selfishness and so much more.

May you know the glory of repentance! Do not be afraid of it. Repentance is the act of expressing sorrowful regret to God and turning away from sinful thoughts and behaviors. It will bring forgiveness, freedom and a hope-filled future.

No one likes to hear that they are a "sinner" or that they "sin". But God saw the status of mankind as lost and rebellious sinners, so He gave the world Jesus Christ to change their perilous end. It's total love. Pure. Unconditional. Miraculous.

May you recognize Jesus Christ loves you, start with that. His love was proven by His death on the cross, and His power was proven by His resurrection (and much more). He offers a call for you to come to Him for the forgiveness of all your sins (past, present, future), and to place your faith in Him for every day and every decision of your life.

He offers you a cleansing wash that will put you in right standing with God. It's through the blood that Jesus shed as he was dying for the world, that will make you as white as snow. It's a God-thing . . . not of our efforts, only His.

May you come to him as you are. Come broken and bleeding. Come humble and needy. He offers you His pardon for all your misdeeds. He offers you power to overcome the things that hold you captive. He offers you the Holy Spirit and its fruit, like love, joy, peace, and more. All the good things. He promises to help you through the rough times, lead you though the confusing times, and bless you at all times.

May you absorb the truth that Jesus when Jesus died, He paid sin's ransom. He took your sin's penalty of death as His own, exchanging your fate of eternal hell for an eternal life with Him as your Savior.

May you see that Heaven is for people who choose to believe in His Son, Jesus Christ, and place their faith completely in Him. It is not hard or a thing of grief. It's a thing of grace. God Himself will lead you there . . . to that place of spirit and soul refreshment. Take a drink of His Living Water.

Ahhh . . . refreshment, restoration, rest.

Meditation

Repent, therefore, and return, that your sins may be wiped away, in order that times of refreshing may come from the presence of the Lord, and that he may send Jesus, the Christ appointed for you.

1. From where does all spiritual refreshment originate? _____

    _____

2. Do you need spiritual refreshment? _____

3. Who is sent to you when you repent and return? _____

4. Is there anyone who has not sinned (not including Jesus)? (Romans 3:23) _____

5. What caused death in the first place? (Romans 6:23) _____

6. What is the gift of God? (I John 1:9-10) _____

7. How do you get cleansed from your sins? _____

    _____

8. What is the status of your relationship with God after He saves you? (Isaiah 1:18) _____

9. What is Jesus doing now for you? (John 14:1-6) _____

    _____

Prayer

My Marvelous Father,

From before the foundations of the earth, you had me on your mind! You chose to send your Son to earth and provide me a way to live forever! What a supernatural gift of love and grace!

It is so completely perfect and is for someone as imperfect as me. You overwhelm me, Jesus, that you would take such cruel torture for someone as flawed as me. How you love me!

Here I am - just as I am. I am a sinner in need of a Savior; I am a lost sheep in need of a Shephard; I am a broken vessel in need of a Healer.

I take you as my Savior, and accept the gift of forgiveness that you have prepared for me. How wonderful it is to no longer try to be good enough for you!

I take you as my Shepherd, and ask you to guide me always.

I take you as my Healer, and ask you to heal my broken body and soul.

I give you my life. Fill me with your Holy Spirit and guide me all through my life until I pass from this earth into the place you have prepared for me.

In the name of the most beautiful Savior, Jesus. Amen.

Day 30

Leaving a Legacy

Blessing

May you leave a fragrant legacy of God's love today, tomorrow and forever. May this be the aroma of Christ settling over you and permeating your world. We all leave a legacy of one kind or another, and after we are no longer present on earth, our families, friends, and acquaintances, will remember our being, our commitments and our character.

May you take time to think about what remains in any given space when you leave. Have you spoken kind and encouraging words, or did you leave an odor of bitterness, negativity or death? Did you curse or bless? Did you love or hate? Did anyone learn that you know God's love? All these things leave an after-waft in the minds and hearts of people who hear and experience you.

May you take the time to ponder your life-time legacy. Will there be a lingering trace of grace long after you're gone? Will there be a remembrance of forgiveness, generosity, humility and strength in the hearts of loved ones and your community?

Most of all, will there be an inheritance of your love for your Savior, Jesus Christ, and your relationship with Him? You see, the more you stay in a love-relationship with the Father, Son and Holy Spirit, the more you effuse His beautiful character everywhere.

May you pursue love, know it and live it. May you fill your spaces with the very character of Christ. Do this not out of duty, for there is no pleasantry in that. It will come naturally as you enjoy God, delighting in His forgiveness and goodness to you. Ah, take a whiff. He loves you.

Meditation

Ephesians 5:1-2 *Therefore, be imitators of God, as beloved children, and walk in love, just as Christ also loves you, and gave Himself up for us, an offering and a sacrifice to God, as a fragrant aroma.*

1. How is Jesus' death on the cross described in this passage?

   _____

   _____

2. With what characteristics are we to walk out our faith? _____

   _____

II Corinthians 2:14-17

3. Who is responsible for spreading the fragrance of the knowledge of Jesus Christ? _____

4. How are believers described to people who are saved and who are perishing? _____

5. Are we sufficient for these things by ourselves? _____

6. Who has called and equipped us to be the fragrance of the knowledge of Christ? _____

Prayer

Oh, Great and Mighty God,

I delight in you and worship you as my one true God. You are the one who called me and the one who saved me. I worship you as the Creator and the giver of life and love. You are precious beyond words. You are the very scent of life to me.

Thank you for Jesus' sacrifice and offering of His life as a fragrant aroma to God. Thank you for your call to be an imitator of Christ and to be a sweet perfume of love to the world.

I desire to be the fragrance of Christ always. Each day I want to walk in the beauty of your love and spread the sweet bouquet of blessing to all I meet. May my life be one that is absent of the putrid things of this world, and filled only with the beauty of living fully for you.

And when I pass from this earth, may my legacy be marked only by the sweet aroma of God's love. May the remembrance of me be that of my Savior's precious presence ever in me.

In the lovely name of Jesus, Amen.

Day 31

A Friend to the End

Blessing

May you be blessed by extraordinary friendships. Throughout your life may you possess precious memories of God-knit connections that make your whole soul smile. And may your friends' memories of you be of the same sentiment.

May you write on the pages of your heart the characteristics that make for true friendship, and live by those standards. Look first unto Jesus Christ, the friend of sinners. He loves <u>unconditionally</u>. He loves <u>constantly</u>, and He loves <u>compassionately</u>.

May you know Jesus as a friend who loves you just as you are. He has forgiven all your misdeeds and sees you as completely redeemed by Himself. He invites the forsaken, the lonely, the broken, and the unlovable to sit at the banquet table of friendship and feast forever with him.

May you RSVP immediately with a humble acceptance of his invitation to come and enjoy this life and eternity with Him. No need to clean up, spruce up or fix up for Jesus. He's the one who does the work in you. Just come as you are. As a friend, accept your friends as they are.

May you know Jesus as a faithful friend. Even though you may have strayed away for a long time, you never leave His loving embrace. When

Jesus knew his followers would abandon Him at the time of his deepest trial, the Bible says, "He loved them to the end." As a friend, be faithful.

May you know Jesus as a compassionate friend. While on earth, He was moved by compassion to help or heal someone in need. He saw the distress of the multitudes and felt compassion for that them, for they were 'like sheep without a shepherd'. He fed them, healed them, taught them, and saved them. He does the same today. As a friend, be tender-hearted and loving.

May you be very wise when choosing your friends. Though you love all, the wrong companion can bring you down a path toward destruction. Your confidants, bosom-buddies, your "bestie" all need to be pursuers and carriers of the Spirit of the Living God. Nothing less will do. They will be the ones to lift you when weak, encourage you when weary and guide you when wandering. They will listen well, speak wisely, and pray always. Do the same for them.

May you always imitate Jesus Christ's friendship in all your friendships. Be generous with your time and possessions, be gracious with your words, and be grateful for their presence in your life. Your friends are God's gift to you, and they are to be treasured always.

May you pray for your friends just as Jesus prayed for His disciples, whom He called his Friends. He asked the Father that they would have His joy. May you pray the same for your friends. There is nothing more satisfying and powerful on earth than the sacred joy of Jesus within a man, woman or child. That prayer alone is a great gift, for it encapsulates the very blessings of God.

Meditation

1. How long did Jesus love His disciples? (John 13:1) _____

   _____

2. Who called you into this relationship with Jesus? (I Corinthians 1:9) _____

3. How loyal were the disciples to Jesus? (Mark 14:50) _____

   _____

4. Describe the character of the Lord. (Psalm 100:5) _____

   _____

John 15: 12-17

This is my commandment, that you love one another, just as I have loved you. Greater love has no one than this, that one lay down his life for his friends. You are my friends if you do what I command you. No longer do I call you slaves, for the slave does not know what his master is doing; but I have called you friends, for all things that I have heard from My Father, I have made known to you. You did not choose Me, but I chose you and appointed you that you would go and bear fruit, and that your fruit would remain so that whatever you ask of the Father in My name He may give to you. This I command you, that you love one another.

5. What is the greatest quality of friendship? _____

   _____

6. What is the greatest sacrifice of friendship? _____

   _____

7. How do we demonstrate our friendship back to Jesus? _____

   _____

<u>Isaiah 54:10</u>

"For the mountains may be moved, and the hills may shake, but My lovingkindness to you and My covenant of peace will not be shaken", *says the Lord who has compassion on you.*

    8.   When your world falls apart, how will the Lord act towards you? _____

    9.   What never changes? _____

   10. In what would a believer have hope? (<u>Lamentations 3:21-23</u>)

             _____

   11. What is another name for God? (<u>I Thessalonians 5:24</u>)

             _____

   12. Is God faithful to forgive sins? (<u>I John 1:9</u>) _____

   13. Examine your friendships. Have you always been loving? (<u>Proverbs 17:17</u>) _____

          Thoughts: _____

             _____

   14. What can you do to improve the quality of your friendships?

             _____

             _____

             _____

Prayer

Dear Jesus,

You are the dearest friend I have ever known. You left Heaven, became a human, took cruel abuses and surrendered to a torturous death to ensure a forever friendship with me. You are kind, compassionate, faithful and true. You take me just as I am and desire my friendship, even though I deserve nothing.

Your friendship never leaves me. When others turn on me, you turn toward me. You invite me into your care and keeping, even though I run renegade at times. Your forgiveness overwhelms me. You supply me with gifts and graces that bless me beyond my ability to understand. You get excited about me, and can't wait to hear my voice in your ear. Thank you for having me always on your mind!

I thank you for the friends you have given to me, and I ask for the ability to love them like you love me. Remove from me any judgement, criticism, or short-comings I may have as a friend, and supply me with the compassion, understanding, faithfulness and the kindness of Christ, so that I may pass it on to the world around me.

In the name of Jesus, my forever friend, Amen.

About the Author

Teresa Nelson has spent her life helping people. Her passion is to give people the tools and the truth they need to succeed in this life; and even more so, to guide them to a passionate, joyful experience of God now and forever.

Currently, Teresa serves as a community pastor, a professional speaker, a teacher in corrections, an auctioneer, and an actor. Previously, she has worked as a case manager, an executive director of a Christian ministry, and grant specialist. She believes all these roles have brought her to this point of penning what she believes people need spiritually, and earnestly prays that her words would bring present and eternal benefit to those who would read them.

She has been married to Steve for 42 years, and both are thrilled with their four grown children, their loving spouses and nine beautiful grandchildren. For good times, Teresa and her family enjoy camping, country living, and all the wildlife roaming their fields.

For refreshment, Teresa delights in drinking very good coffee, while engaging in great conversation with exceptionally grand friends.